2 IN THE MIDDLE

THOMAS J. BYE

Prentice Hall Regents
Englewood Cliffs, New Jersey

Bye, Thomas.
In the middle / Thomas Bye, Ph.D
p. cm.
Includes an unnumbered introductory v. entitled Newcomer.
ISBN 0-13-454398-X. -- ISBN 0-13-454224-X (bk. 1). -- ISBN 0-13-454265-7 (bk. 2). -- ISBN 0-13-454307-6 (bk. 3)
1. English language--Textbooks for foreign speakers. I. Title.
PE1128.B862 1996
428.2'4--dc20 95-5232
CIP

Manager of Development Services: *Louisa B. Hellegers*
Development Editors: *Tünde A. Dewey, Gino Mastascusa, Kathleen Schultz*
Audio Development Editor: *D. Andrew Gitzy*
Directors of Production and Manufacturing: *Aliza Greenblatt David Riccardi*
Production Editors and Compositors: *Wanda España, Christine McLaughlin Mann*
Production Assistant: *Kelly Tavares*
Production Coordinators: *Dave Dickey, Ray Keating*
Art Director: *Paul Belfanti*
Page Design/Storyboards for Electronic Background Paintings: *Anna Veltfort*
Rendering of Electronic Background Paintings: *Rolando Corujo, Anna Veltfort*
Scanning and Electronic Art Production Manager: *Todd Ware*
Electronic Art Production: *Marita Froimson*
Electronic Art Production Assistant: *Don Kilcoyne*
Realia Coordinator: *Wanda España*
Photographer: *Ken Karp Photography, Inc.*
Photo Researcher: *Kathy Ringrose*
Cover Designers: *Paul Belfanti, Wanda España*
Design Concept: *Paula Maylahn*
Interior Design: *Curriculum Concepts, Inc.*

Prentice-Hall, Inc.
A Division of Simon & Schuster
Englewood Cliffs, New Jersey 07632

Printed in the United States of America

10 9 8 7 6 5 4 3 2 1

ISBN 0-13-454265-7 (paper)
0-13-213802-6 (case)

Prentice-Hall International (UK) Limited, London
Prentice-Hall of Australia Pty. Limited, Sydney
Prentice-Hall Canada Inc., Toronto
Prentice-Hall Hispanoamericana, S.A., Mexico
Prentice-Hall of India Private Limited, New Delhi
Prentice-Hall of Japan, Inc., Tokyo
Simon & Schuster Asia Pte. Ltd., Singapore
Editora Prentice-Hall do Brasil, Ltda., Rio de Janeiro

INTRODUCTION

TO THE STUDENT

Welcome to **IN THE MIDDLE**. This book is written just for you! **IN THE MIDDLE** will help you learn English *naturally*, as you take part in activities that keep you talking . . . doing . . . and thinking — all while you are having fun.

This year you'll learn even more about your school and what it takes to be a good student. You'll talk about issues and concerns that are on the minds of other kids your age. You'll work with others to make sense of the world around you. You'll show others what you know and what you can do. You'll learn more about your school. You'll learn more about what to do and who to see if you have a problem or need help.

You'll also learn new ideas and words that will help you in your other classes and outside the classroom. You'll use new math skills and learn more about science. You'll learn about your neighborhood and the world around you. Best of all, you'll work with others. And . . . you'll learn English!

By the end of Level 2, you will be ready to communicate in English for a variety of purposes. You will be able to

- converse more fluently with others;
- function confidently outside the classroom;
- express your feelings, thoughts and opinions;
- explore and discuss the world around you;
- take an active part in lessons in other classes;
- work with others to learn;
- be a success in school.

You'll also continue to read and write in English. Your writer's **Portfolio** will give you a chance to share your thoughts and show what you know. You'll read poems that kids your age have written and you'll connect their ideas to your own life.

This is going to be a great year! Have fun!

TO THE TEACHER

Welcome to **IN THE MIDDLE**, a comprehensive English language program that makes the classroom come alive. Responding to the unique developmental needs of young adolescents, every lesson promotes active learning and helps create an interactive classroom environment.

IN THE MIDDLE provides a student-centered perspective that reflects the personal and social concerns of today's adolescents. **IN THE MIDDLE** treats students as thinkers whose emerging ideas about the world are to be respected and valued. Students' knowledge, experiences, and interests help set the classroom agenda.

Lessons engage students in situations and experiences that stimulate discovery and discussion. Students have opportunities to express their own ideas and to hear and reflect on the ideas of others. Lessons provide students with opportunities to initiate their own learning. Open-ended activities give students the chance to think for themselves, make choices, and give input based on their lives and backgrounds.

The themes and topics of **IN THE MIDDLE** are aligned with current middle-level curriculum initiatives that promote understanding of the language in context. Task-based activities develop critical and creative thinking skills.

Students make connections of language and context across the curriculum. Lessons give students concepts, terminology, strategies, and skills they need for success in other classes. Students also learn how to learn. They reflect on their own habits of thinking and learning. They work at becoming strategic, independent learners.

Incorporating a communicative methodology, **IN THE MIDDLE** promotes acquisition through a content-based curriculum that is determined by the unique academic and social needs — and interests — of students in the middle grades. Materials develop both everyday language skills and the language proficiency needed for success in the classroom.

Themes and language forms are recycled; lessons make increasingly complex language demands of the student that are age- and stage-appropriate. Authentic language in context and lavish use of illustrations and realia provide students with comprehensible input.

Every unit integrates listening, speaking, reading, and writing and promotes interaction, thinking, and negotiation of meaning. Although grammar and vocabulary are introduced in context, language forms are not overtly practiced. Rather, grammatical structures, notions, functions, and vocabulary emerge naturally from the content focus of each lesson. Language use develops through meaning and understanding.

Finally students learn that working together works. A variety of activities involve students in learning cooperatively with partners and in groups. Projects and hands-on activities ensure high levels of interaction and create student motivation and feelings of success and competence.

IN THE MIDDLE is organized in four developmental levels.

▲ **THE NEWCOMER LEVEL** helps newly arrived students develop emergent and beginning reading and writing skills — and includes special support for the "silent-period" student.

▲ **LEVEL 1** enables students to move from the early-production stage to the extended-production stage of language development.

▲ **LEVEL 2** is designed for students who are beginning to communicate fluently and use language creatively.

▲ **LEVEL 3** prepares students for transition to the regular instructional program by engaging them in tasks that demand increasingly complex oral and written communication.

Let's take a closer look at Level 2. Level 2 is designed for students who are beginning to communicate fluently and use language creatively. By the end of Level 2 students will be producing increasingly elaborate utterances and will be able to communicate in settings with less and less contextual support. They will function across a variety of social situations. They will demonstrate that they are increasingly capable readers and writers.

Organized around a rich array of student-centered themes, Level 2 engages students in a variety of activity- and project-based learning experiences that promote interaction, thinking, and discussion. Level 2 methodology extends Level 1 activities by giving greater attention to open-ended discussion, role play, problem-solving, interviewing, and the use of a variety of literature to prompt thinking and writing. **IN THE MIDDLE** helps students become enthusiastic readers and effective writers. Students learn to read by reading. They learn to write by writing.

A writer's **Portfolio** extends the **Student Book**. The **Portfolio** helps students develop as writers, engaging them in a variety of activities that include expressive, descriptive, persuasive, informative, and real-world writing. Grammar and writing skills are embedded in writing activities that encourage students to write for different purposes and audiences. Each Level 2 unit in the **Portfolio** includes six activities.

An **Audio Program** develops listening comprehension skills. Students listen and respond to authentic conversations recorded by professional actors.

The **Teacher's Resource Manual** provides straightforward procedures for using each program component. Step-by-step instructions for the **Student Book** activities and language structure charts are provided. The **Teacher's Resource Manual** is designed to ensure that teachers new to the field will find everything they need to be successful in the classroom. Experienced teachers will discover a wealth of creative teaching ideas for enriching instruction and extending the material on the student pages.

The **Teacher's Resource Manual** also includes:

- A complete **tapescript** for the listening activities included in the Audio Program;
- **Reproducible Blackline Masters** such as a concept web and a homework schedule, which enhance the hands-on approach to active participation in class.
- A **Family Links** section, which provides suggestions for strengthening the ties between the school and home. This section includes unit ideas for involving parents and family members in classroom activities.
- A **Literature Links** section, which suggests titles in English that teachers might wish to include in their classroom libraries to extend the theme and topics of each unit in the **Student Book** and are appropriate to the students' level of proficiency.
- A **Portfolio Assessment Program**, which enables teachers to evaluate each student's oral and written language development. All assessments elicit student-constructed responses and have an authentic focus. Because the assessment of reading and writing is embedded in the **Portfolio**, the teacher and student can monitor language development on an ongoing, systematic basis. Scoring rubrics allow the teacher to evaluate both the effectiveness and accuracy of student writing.

The **In the Middle Assessment System** consists of a placement instrument and end-of-level assessments. The placement instrument determines each student's initial level of proficiency in English. End-of-level assessments determine performance levels in oral and written language — allowing comparison over time and from student to student.

SCOPE AND

UNIT	THEMES AND INQUIRIES	EVERYDAY COMMUNICATION	LANGUAGE/ VOCABULARY IN CONTEXT
1 There's the Bell!	Institutions: Being part of the school ▲ What classes should I take? ▲ What classes and activities will help me explore my personal interests?	Expressing personal interests Explaining a problem to an adult Making suggestions Telling time	Duration Time-when: *earlier, later* *wh* questions *have . . . don't have any* Temporary present: *-ing* School subjects, clubs, and after-school activities Naming musical instruments
2 You Must Be Homesick!	Transitions: Fitting in in a new school ▲ How can I meet new friends? ▲ Who at school can help me? ▲ How will I find my way around school? ▲ What are the rules and expectations? ▲ What if I break a rule? ▲ Are there incentives for good behavior? ▲ What can I do for fun at school?	Introductions Expressing worries and concerns Starting a conversation with a stranger Making small talk Talking about likes and dislikes: *favorite/least favorite* Giving directions	*wh* questions *How long . . . ?* Location Possibility: *if . . . you can* The language of school rules
3 Why Don't You Sleep Over?	Interdependence: Life in a large family ▲ What is a family tree? ▲ Who are the members of my family? ▲ What is daily life like in a large family?	Describing people Formal vs. informal Introductions Compliments and criticisms Requests made in varying degrees of politeness Telling how to set the dinner table Making conversation at the dinner table	Age: Comparison (*younger, youngest, older, oldest, same age as . . .*) Present habit: *always, usually* Location: *to the right, to the left, next to, between, on top of, under . . .* Condition: *unless* Possession: *my, mine, Trevor's, belongs to . . .* Kinship terms Personality traits and personal qualities Foods Dishes and utensils Bedroom furnishings Sports equipment Boy's clothing

SEQUENCE

LEARNING WITH OTHERS	CONTENT CONNECTIONS	READING AND WRITING
Sharing and comparing class schedules Making "dream" schedules and requirements for middle school	Course requirements School electives After-school activities Clubs	Reading for detail: *what*, *where*, and *when* Reading schedules Reading descriptions (courses, clubs) Making a timeline Interviewing a teacher and writing a profile Writing a paragraph about a subject in school Responding to a poem by writing a letter to a school counselor Making a poster or flyer Drawing a picture and writing a short paragraph
Designing an incentives program for good behavior Using a school map	The Student Handbook School rules	Reading a school map Reading a table of contents Reading about an event in the school newspaper Keeping a personal journal Responding to a poem by drawing a picture and writing an account of a past event Making a poster about lunch rules at school Writing a conversation Interviewing a student and writing a profile Writing questions to match answers already given Writing a letter to a friend
Drawing a family tree		Describing a room Interviewing a family member and writing his or her story Responding to a short story by drawing a picture and writing a description about an actual experience Completing a Venn diagram and writing a related description Finishing a note Making a list and writing about the most important thing on the list

UNIT	THEMES AND INQUIRIES	EVERYDAY COMMUNICATION	LANGUAGE/ VOCABULARY IN CONTEXT
4 Let's Check Out the Exhibits!	Wellness: Making healthy choices ▲ Do I have a healthy lifestyle? ▲ How can I eat right? ▲ How can I take care of my teeth? ▲ What's wrong with smoking? ▲ When should I see a doctor?	Understanding an explanation: how a cavity is formed Following step-by-step instructions (for brushing and flossing) Reporting a health problem Asking advice	*About* Present habit Past sequence of events Amount: *more, less* Negative condition: *unless* Direction: *up and down, back and forth, at an angle, in a circle* Location: *against, around* Terms related to height and weight Healthy and unhealthy foods Physical symptoms Over-the-counter medicines
5 Could You Lend Me Some Money	Consumerism: Surviving in the market place ▲ What kind of gift should I buy? ▲ What can I afford? ▲ What are my own preferences? ▲ How do I make a purchase? ▲ How can I get the best price?	Requesting Making suggestions Giving advice Expressing needs and wants Making a purchase Buying things on sale Counting out money, change	Amount: *enough, plenty, not enough, too little, more than enough* Conditional would Location *This, that, these, those* Pronoun *one* Comparison: *more than, less than* Prominence: *This is the one I want.* Approximation: *about* Degree: *too, enough* Intensity: *sort of, kind of, not much, not at all, really, very* Kitchen items Audio equipment Height and weight terms Clothing sizes and labels
6 I Wonder What They Would Say About Us!	Identities: Group and cultural identity Institutions: Cultural differences and diversity in school and society ▲ What group(s) do I belong to? How am I like the other members of my group? ▲ What do we mean by "culture?" ▲ What is the ethnic make-up of my community? ▲ What languages are spoken in the United States and in my community? ▲ How well do I speak English?	Expressing similarities and differences Using body language to express meaning, feelings, and attitudes	Expressing number: *one in six, many, half, most, a few, a third, increasing, decreasing* Place: *from Asia to Seattle* Amount: *count* and *non-count nouns* Nationalities

Learning with Others	Content Connections	Reading and Writing
Choosing a healthy diet Discussing poor eating habits Making and sharing a poster about the hazards of smoking	Physical education: "You are what you eat."	Interpreting a height and weight chart Understanding written information and advice about health Interpreting information in a graph Reading warning labels Interviewing an adult about lifestyle and writing a profile Making a food log and diary Responding to a poem by making a collage Making an anti-smoking ad Listing suggestions to help a person stop smoking Drawing a cartoon about a medical emergency
Managing allowances Estimating sale prices Comparing recorded estimations Comparing birthdays from different cultures	Math: Estimating	Writing a description (of how someone is dressed) Writing a thank-you letter Listing weekly expenses and writing a letter to parents asking for a bigger allowance Reading about how a can opener works and then writing about how an object at home works Writing a story about buying a piece of clothing and then regretting it later Responding to a piece of writing by identifying the descriptive words in the writing Making estimations and recording them in a log
Summarizing information Making charts Making posters Drawing pictures to show body language Making a timeline about the history of a community Observing body language other people use	Social Studies: The ethnic make-up of the United States Talking about immigration Discussing different cultures	Reading a map Reading text for information Identifying words borrowed into English from Native American languages Writing something for an imaginary time capsule Writing a paragraph about the history of one's community Responding to a news article by stating one's opinion Responding to an essay by identifying places on a map whose names come from different cultures Reading a recipe and then writing one that reflects one's own culture

UNIT	THEMES AND INQUIRIES	EVERYDAY COMMUNICATION	LANGUAGE/ VOCABULARY IN CONTEXT
7 I Want to Be a Better Student!	Success and competence: Study strategies and skills ▲ How good are my study and homework habits? ▲ How can I get the most out of reading my textbook? ▲ How can I use what I already know to learn? ▲ How can I organize what I am learning so that I can use the information later?	Giving step-by-step directions Following step-by-step directions for making something Making excuses Giving advice	Frequency: *rarely, sometimes, often, always* *When* clauses Present habit Cause: *because* clauses Transition words: sequence in time Amount: *any* in a question Past events: irregular verbs
8 Let's Have a Party for Juan!	Caring: Sustaining friendships Recognizing and avoiding barriers to communication (put-downs, gossip, and other conversation stoppers) Understanding the rules of a game ▲ If I'm invited to a party, how should I behave? ▲ If I'm invited to a party, how should I behave? ▲ What should I say? When is it time to leave? ▲ What can I do to work with others? ▲ What can I do to get along with others?	Asking permission Communicating effectively in a group Sustaining a conversation Deciding Giving advice and making suggestions Apologizing Complimenting and criticizing Describing floor plans	Parts of a textbook Reported discourse: *He'll say I'm too young.* Future events: *will, won't* Past events Completed actions vs. actions yet to be completed: *already . . . still have to* Comparison: *larger, largest* Party items
9 What Are Families for, Anyway?	Interdependence: family responsibilities ▲ What household jobs should I be responsible for doing? ▲ How do I feel about male and female roles? ▲ What do I consider to be work and what do I consider to be fun?	Requesting: *Could you . . . ?* Ordering (someone to do something): *Somebody needs to empty the garbage.* Volunteering: *I'll water the plants.* Giving directions (for doing something) Thanking	Temporary events: *She's making our lunches.* Quantifier pronouns: *somebody, anybody* Conditional *if* clauses *-ing* nominals in subject position Embedded *how* questions: *I don't know how . . .* Degree: *too young to . . .* Household tasks Adjectives that describe household jobs Household tools

LEARNING WITH OTHERS	CONTENT CONNECTIONS	READING AND WRITING
Understanding and demonstrating directions for making something Making charts and graphs Making homework schedules Interviewing classmates	Discussing study habits	Strategies for reading a textbook for understanding: Before, during, and after reading Organizing information: Making a concept web Understanding parts of a textbook Understanding tables and graphs Outlining strategies Taking good notes Understanding and using proofreading symbols Editing for form Responding to a survey about teachers by describing the ideal teacher Responding to a student's note by stating one's own ideas Writing a letter to a publisher Writing an essay Making a timeline and writing an entry in a diary
Working in groups Drawing a map to one's home Playing games Planning a party with family members Sharing a birthday card of one's own culture with classmates		Reading a neighborhood map and following written directions Reading floor plans Words and syllables Rhyme ("sounds like") Books that teens enjoy Recognizing humor Writing a letter to one's mother Drawing a map and writing directions Writing a humorous conversation Responding to a short story by writing an essay Designing a birthday card
Understanding information presented in a table Making graphs and tables to present information Interviewing an adult family member about his or her responsibilities Comparing interview results with classmates	Designing a survey	Writing a description that requires careful observation Simile Rewriting dialogs Responding to a poem by writing one's own poem using similar elements Responding to a poem by writing an editorial for the school newspaper Reading a survey about house chores and deciding which chore is the least favorite Writing a note to an adult family member Writing a "how-to" essay

UNIT	THEMES AND INQUIRIES	EVERYDAY COMMUNICATION	LANGUAGE/ VOCABULARY IN CONTEXT
10 What's Happening to My Body?	Wellness: Growing bodies need exercise and good food ▲ In what ways is my body changing? Am I normal? ▲ What does it mean to eat well? ▲ How fit am I? ▲ Why is exercise good for me? How often should I exercise? What kinds of exercise should I do?	Giving advice Making suggestions Evaluating a diet and designing a healthy menu Designing and evaluating an extensive program	Comparison: *taller, later, deeper, greater, etc.* Group membership: *belongs to* Addition: *so does, so do* *-ing* nominals as subjects and objects Conditional *if* clauses: *If I'm going to job, I'll need . . .* Amounts and measures: *three ounces, half a cup* Foods Body parts Exercise clothing and equipment
11 This Is My Family!	Identity: Family structures, rules, and roles ▲ What about family rules? ▲ What are my own family's values? How can culture affect family values? ▲ How are families the same—and how are they different? ▲ How traditional is my family? How are families changing? ▲ What are the responsibilities of people in my family? ▲ How does my family spend time together?	Interviewing other people	Composition: *consists of, includes, has, is a member of* Manner: *-ing* nominals after *for* and *by*: *I help by taking care of my sister. I'm responsible for taking care of my sister* Time-when: *When I was younger . . .* Past habit vs. present habit: *I used to . . ./Now I . . .* Negative present habit: *don't any more* Obligation + condition: *I have to wash the dishes before I can . . .* Permission: *I can . . .*
12 This is an Emergency!	Wellness: Safety and first aid ▲ Do I know what to do in an emergency? ▲ How can I prevent home accidents? ▲ What do I do to get help?	Warning, prohibition Making an emergency call for help	Past progressive: *We were riding our skateboards when . . .* Reported speech: *I said, "Let's get the custodian."* Hypothetical event: *If I were stung by a bee, I would . . .* Present state: *There are toys on the stairs. The lamp cord is frayed. . . .* Cause: *Cleaning fluid makes you dizzy.* Items in a first aid kit Household cleaning products

LEARNING WITH OTHERS	CONTENT CONNECTIONS	READING AND WRITING
Designing a healthy menu Comparing eating habits Talking about the benefits of exercise Making a poster Describing how the body works	Physical education: Exercise and fitness Healthy diet Developing a personal exercise program Keeping a learning log in one subject Parts of the human body	Understanding a visual (food pyramid) Interpreting data in a table Responding to a poem about PE class by writing a page in one's journal Writing a summary of the lesson on good health Writing a "restaurant review" of one's school cafeteria Responding to an advertisement by improving the ad Responding to a concrete poem by writing a new one
Turning survey data into visual form Reflecting on the values of one's family Comparing families Planning a television show Writing a TV script with family members Writing a letter of advice to a classmate Discussing with family most important values	Understanding information in a column graph	Persuasive writing: TV commercial Humorous writing: making a poster about how to survive a family vacation Writing interview questions Writing a program description for TV Guide Responding to a poem about being a young adolescent Making a chart to compare two families and writing a related paragraph Responding to a poem by writing one's own experiences and observations Making a concept web Writing a letter to an advice columnist Making a chart about making decisions in a family Writing a letter to parents requesting more authority
Taking a quiz Learning first aid procedures Demonstrating the Heimlich Maneuver Interviewing an adult at school about safety procedures Deciding with friends what to include in a "wilderness survival kit" Comparing survival kits with classmates Listing all safety hazards at school Making a list of questions about safety	Physical education: Wellness and first aid	Writing an eyewitness account of an event Understanding step-by-step procedures Reading safety labels Writing about school safety procedures Reading a get-well card and then designing one's own Writing a letter to one's principal about safety hazards at school Making a poster about home safety Writing a letter of invitation

UNIT	THEMES AND INQUIRIES	EVERYDAY COMMUNICATION	LANGUAGE/ VOCABULARY IN CONTEXT
13 You're Old Enough to Find a Part-time Job!	Consumerism: The pressure to find work ▲ Should I get a part-time job? What are the pros and cons? ▲ How would I balance a job and school? ▲ How would I find a part-time job? ▲ What kinds of jobs would suit me? ▲ What about job interviewing skills?	Requesting Expressing personal interests Interviewing for a part-time job Giving advice Offering feedback: *You should have . . . shouldn't have . . .* How body language conveys attitudes Explaining	Degree: *not old enough; too young* Reason: *because* Condition + possibility: *If you like working outdoors, then you might enjoy shoveling snow.* Narrative present Past events Personal qualities
14 Maybe You Should Run For Office!	Institutions: Running for office to make school a better place ▲ What kind of student government does my school have? ▲ Why do people run for office? ▲ How does a candidate get on the ballot? ▲ What are ballot measures? ▲ How does a candidate persuade the voters? ▲ How do I go about voting?	Making suggestions Promising: *If you elect me, I'll . . .* Advising: *You'll need . . .* Convincing others Telling what you are for and against	Hypothetical states: *If I were an officer, I would . . .* Prohibition: *may not . . . , must not . . ., is not allowed . . .* Comparison: *smarter than, as smart as, smartest* Amount: *most, many, some, a few, hardly anyone, only a few, almost nobody . . .* Terms describing the qualities of a leader Terms describing positive qualities in people

Learning with Others	Content Connections	Reading and Writing
Interviewing Discussing advantages and disadvantages of part-time jobs Interviewing an adult about a part-time job that sounds interesting	Developing a schedule for work, school, and free-time activities Figuring out how to make a business Reflecting on how personal experiences, abilities, and interests relate to work choices	Writing an advertising flyer Writing a personal narrative Responding to a poem about getting a part-time job by writing a letter to one's parents Rewriting a conversation to change the outcome of the situation Writing a resumé
Planning and holding a class election: Nominating candidates, running for office, polling, and voting Judging the qualifications of candidates for office Designing a campaign poster	School government Understanding graphs Presenting information from a table in a graph	Reading a newspaper article (about elections) Interpreting election poll results Writing a biographical sketch of a hero Writing a short biography of a student who would make an ideal leader Making a concept web Making a pros and cons chart Writing a letter to the editor of one's school newspaper concerning a change in school policy Responding to an amusing poem by writing one's own poem, using a similar theme Designing publicity for a friend who is running for office at school Writing a front-page news article about the Kennedy school election

ACKNOWLEDGMENTS

The author would like to thank and acknowledge the following people, whose insights, suggestions and hard work helped shape this project:

David Bohne for his encouragement, enthusiasm, and support; the staff of the San Leandro (California) Community Library for research assistance; Tina Carver for promoting and celebrating the project from beginning to end; Tünde Dewey, Louisa Hellegers, Gino Mastascusa, Tom Dare, Johanna Evans, and all the other folks on the PHR team; and finally, Roger Olsen for his help in launching the project and providing feedback in its initial stages.

ILLUSTRATIONS

Storyboards for electronic background paintings: Anna Veltfort

Rendering of electronic background paintings: Rolando Corujo, Anna Veltfort

Dartmouth Publishing, Inc.: pages 135, 141

Michelle Desveaux: page 78

North Market Street Graphics, Mark Ammerman, Art Director: pages 2, 3, 6, 19, 21, 27, 31, 33, 35, 38, 40, 41, 43, 44, 47, 57, 60, 63, 69, 70, 71, 75, 101, 103, 109, 112, 113, 119, 132, 137, 140, 142, 149, 153, 154, 155, 166

William C. Ober, M.D.: 42

Taurins Design Associates: pages 5, 7, 39, 40, 41, 55, 105, 107, 116, 129, 139, 144, 147, 168

Handwriting samples provided by George Polasky's 7th grade students, Our Lady of Czestochowa, Jersey City, N.J.: Oktawia Wojcik and Sadia Ali

REALIA

Paul Belfanti: pages 7, 17, 20, 34, 38, 55, 56, 62, 73, 78, 80, 102, 107, 119, 160, 165, 167

Wanda España: pages 1, 2, 4 (left), 5, 8 (bottom), 10, 33, 39, 58, 68, 69, 76, 77, 82, 85, 87, 100, 106, 112 (center), 117 (top), 118, 120, 121, 125, 126, 127, 128, 129, 130, 131, 134, 136, 138, 139, 140, 146, 147, 148, 149, 150, 151, 153, 156, 158, 163

Ken Liao: pages 4 (right), 8 (top), 9, 11, 16, 21, 29, 36, 46, 50, 59, 66, 74, 81, 83, 88, 98, 105, 114, 122, 151, 161.

Lido Graphics: 3, 6, 14, 17, 22, 47, 51, 67, 72, 81, 86, 95, 101, 104, 117 (bottom), 124, 159, 162

Siren Design: pages 15, 23, 24, 26, 43, 45, 48, 65, 76 (map), 79, 84, 90, 91, 113, 115, 143

PHOTOS

Photographer: Ken Karp Photography, Inc.
Stylist: Jozee Friedrich
Additional Photography: Steven Carr

PERMISSIONS

Page 39: Adapted with permission from "Average Height-Weight Tables for Boys and Girls" from *Nutritional Support of Medical Practice*. Edited by Howard A. Schneider and others. Hagerstown; pages 104 and 127: *The Quicksilver Years, the Hopes and Fears of Early Adolescence*, Search Institute; page 129: From *Love Me, When I Am Most Unlovable*, National Association of Secondary School Principles.

REVIEWERS AND CONSULTANTS

Prentice Hall Regents would like to thank the following reviewers of **IN THE MIDDLE**, whose comments and suggestions have helped to shape the content and format of the series: Rick Amstutz, ESL Teacher, Pinellas County, Florida; Susan Dunlap, Program Assistant, Bilingual/ELD Staff Development, West Contra Costa, California; Reisa Freehling, ESL Coordinator, Bainbridge Island, Washington; Paige Oliver, Crystal Beach, Florida; Ray Ramirez, ESL Teacher/State Trainer, St. Lucie, Florida; Debra Schwabbe, ESL Teacher, Franklin J.H.S., Hillsborough County, Tampa, Florida; Steve Sloan, ESL Coordinator, James Monroe H.S., North Hills, California.

UNIT 1

THERE'S THE BELL!

Chip: Hi, Lori!
Lori: Hi, Chip!
Chip: What are you taking this semester?
Lori: Well, I hope I get ceramics.

Juan: Hi, Shelley!
Shelley: Hi, Juan!
Juan: There's the bell. We have to go to homeroom.
Shelley: Who's your homeroom teacher?
Juan: Let me check the schedule. Let's see . . . my homeroom teacher is . . .

GRADE 7 • HOMEROOM SCHEDULE

Student's Last Name:	Teacher	Room
A, B	Anderson	23
C, D	Chavez	10
E, F, G	Delgado	11
H, I, J	Goldstein	19
K, L	Lim	22
M, N, O, P	Reed	31
Q, R, S	Malkovich	28
T, U, V	Turner	8
W, X, Y, Z	White	34

TUNING IN.

Look at the homeroom schedule. As you hear each student's last name, point to the name of that student's homeroom teacher.

LISTENING IN.

READING ALOUD.

Read the new bell schedule.

NEW BELL SCHEDULE

Homeroom	8:15 – 8:35
Period 1	8:40 – 9:30
Period 2	9:35 – 10:25
Period 3	10:30 – 11:20
Period 4	11:25 – 12:15
LUNCH	12:20 – 12:55
Period 5	1:00 – 1:50
Period 6	1:55 – 2:45

50 minutes long

35 minutes long

TALKING IT OVER. Look at each clock. Tell how long each period of time is.

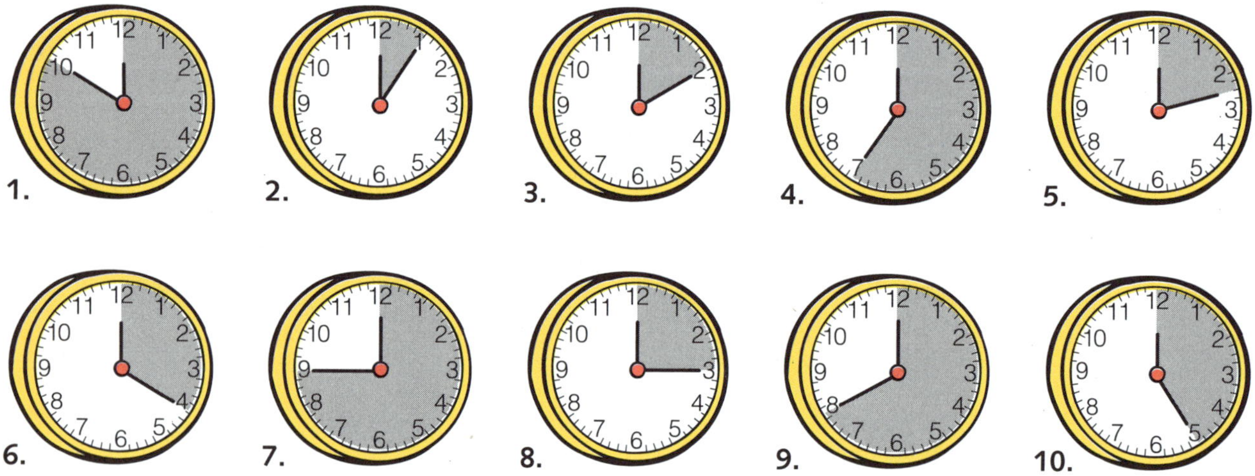
1. 2. 3. 4. 5.
6. 7. 8. 9. 10.

TUNING IN. Listen to Ms. Reed. Point to the clock that shows the time period Ms. Reed is talking about.

FIGURING IT OUT. Work with a partner. Compare the two bell schedules.

longer lunch last year

shorter lunch this year

classes ended later last year

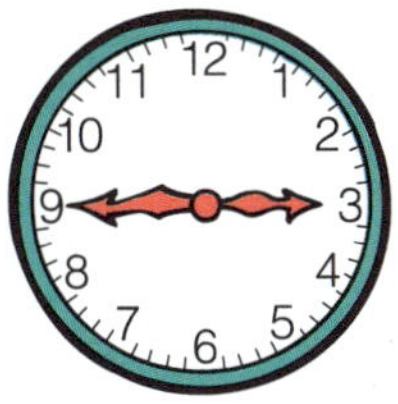

classes end earlier this year

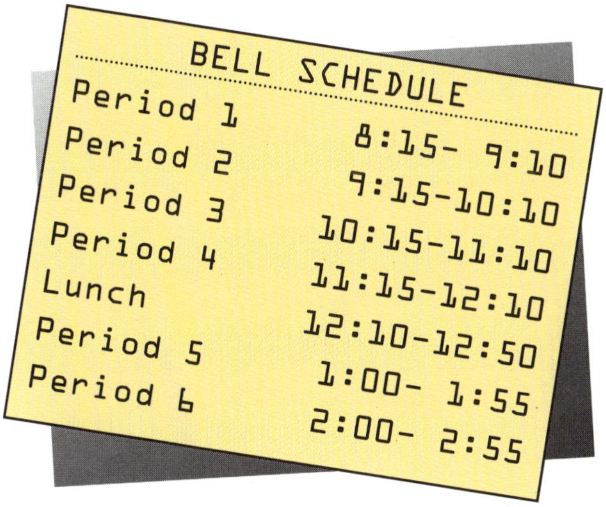

BELL SCHEDULE

Period 1	8:15- 9:10
Period 2	9:15-10:10
Period 3	10:15-11:10
Period 4	11:15-12:10
Lunch	12:10-12:50
Period 5	1:00- 1:55
Period 6	2:00- 2:55

TALKING IT OVER. Compare your school's daily schedule with Kennedy Middle School's daily schedule. Answer these questions with a partner.

1. Does your school day begin earlier or later?
2. Does your school day end earlier or later?
3. Is your lunch period longer or shorter?
4. Are your class periods longer or shorter?

JUST FOR Fun

Work with a partner. Create a "dream schedule" for your school. Think about these questions.

- ▲ What time does school begin and end?
- ▲ How many periods are there?
- ▲ How long is each period?
- ▲ How long is lunch?

Write your dream schedule on a piece of paper. Then share it with your classmates.

READING ALOUD. Read Juan's class schedule.

NEW BELL SCHEDULE

Homeroom	8:15 – 8:35
Period 1	8:40 – 9:30
Period 2	9:35 – 10:25
Period 3	10:30 – 11:20
Period 4	11:25 – 12:15
LUNCH	12:20 – 12:55
Period 5	1:00 – 1:50
Period 6	1:55 – 2:45

Ortíz, Juan Carlos Grade 7 Student #003621

Period/Course	Teacher	Room
1. ESL 2	Reed	10
2. World History	Goldstein	2
3. Math 7	Delgado	32
4. Science 7	Yoshida-Johnson	26
5. PE/Health	Fields	Gym
6. Homemaking I	Garcia	25

FIGURING IT OUT. Work with a partner. Ask and answer these questions about Juan's schedule. Then think of other questions to ask.

▲ What is Juan's first-period class?

▲ Who is his second-period teacher?

▲ What room is he in during fourth period?

▲ What class does Mrs. Garcia teach?

▲ Who teaches Science 7?

▲ What is Juan's sixth-period class?

▲ What class does he have right before lunch?

▲ What class does he have right after lunch?

WRITING AND SHARING. Write your class schedule. Then share it with a partner.

TUNING IN. Look at Juan's schedule and the new bell schedule. Listen as Juan talks about his class schedule and the new bell schedule. For each statement, point your thumb up if it is true. Point your thumb down if it is false.

KENNEDY MIDDLE SCHOOL
• COURSE REQUIREMENTS •

Grade 6	Grade 7	Grade 8
Self-contained core:	English 7	English 8
▪ Language Arts	World History	U.S. History
▪ Math	Math 7	Math 8
▪ Social Studies	Science 7	Science 8
▪ Science	PE/Health	PE/Health
PE/Health	Elective(s)	Elective(s)
	(one semester)	(one semester)

THINKING ABOUT IT.

Read Kennedy's course requirements. Then compare Juan's schedule with the grade 7 course requirements. Is Juan taking all the courses he needs to take?

ACTING IT OUT.

Pretend that you are a student at Kennedy. Tell what courses you have to take.

JUST FOR Fun

Work with a partner. Create a "dream" list of course requirements for middle school. Think about these questions.

- ▲ What are the course requirements for sixth grade?
- ▲ What are the course requirements for seventh grade?
- ▲ What are the course requirements for eighth grade?

Write your dream program on a piece of paper. Then share it with your classmates.

LISTENING IN.

What electives are Tran and Zaida taking?

FINDING OUT.

Read the list of electives at Kennedy. Then find out what electives your school offers. Make a list. Are they the same as Kennedy's?

KENNEDY ELECTIVE PROGRAM

Full-Year Courses	Semester Courses
Spanish A	Drama
Spanish B	Introduction to Art
Beginning Band	Drawing and Painting
Intermediate Band	Ceramics I
Beginning Instruments	Ceramics II
Brass Instruments	Keyboarding
Woodwind Instruments	Homemaking I
Percussion Instruments	Homemaking II
LOGO: Computer programming and problem solving	Exploring Technology I
School Office Practice	Exploring Technology II

FIGURING IT OUT.

Name each instrument.

a. cello
b. trumpet
c. clarinet
d. piano
e. drums
f. saxophone
g. flute
h. trombone
i. guitar
j. violin

TUNING IN. Listen as Ms. Reed asks you what electives you would like to take. For each question, point your thumb up for "yes." Point your thumb down for "no."

THINKING ABOUT IT.

Choose an elective for each student. Be ready to explain your choices!

1.

Kelly would like to play the piano.

2.

Ellen is good at math.

3.

José enjoys cooking.

4.

Mike would like to speak Spanish better.

ON YOUR OWN.

Make a chart like this one. List three or four things you are interested in. Then list three or four electives you would like to take.

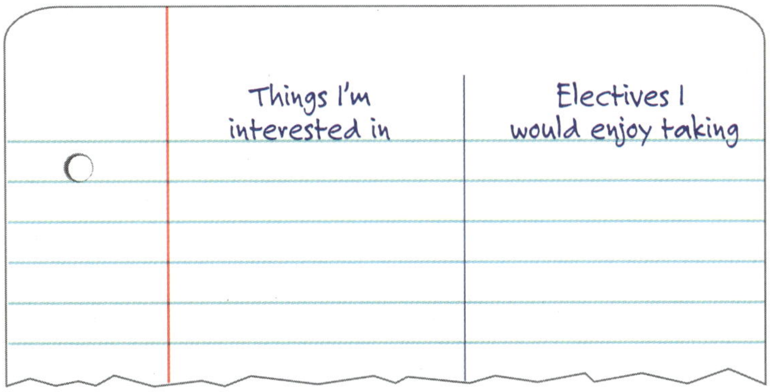

JUST FOR Fun

Draw a picture of yourself in your favorite class. Then share your picture with your classmates. Tell them if the class is a required course or an elective. Explain why it is your favorite class.

LISTENING IN. If students have a problem with their schedules, what do they need to do?

Ms. Reed: Look carefully at your schedules. If you have a problem with your schedule, you'll need to see your counselor. This year, Ms. Vasquez is the seventh-grade counselor.

Miyako: I have two periods of math!

Tran: I don't have a math class!

Juan: My schedule is OK.

FIGURING IT OUT.

Compare Zaida's schedule with the grade 7 course requirements. Make a list of the problems in her schedule.

Pérez, Zaida   Grade 7   Student #003636

Period/Course	Teacher	Room
1. Math 7	Delgado	33
2. Art	Glaze	35
3. Math 7	Chan	33
4. English 8	Wright	17
5. LOGO	Delgado	36

KENNEDY MIDDLE SCHOOL
• COURSE REQUIREMENTS •

Grade 7

1. English 7	4. Science 7
2. World History	5. PE/Health
2. Math 7	6. Elective(s) (one semester)

FIGURING IT OUT. Work in groups of four. Compare these schedules with the grade 7 course requirements. Make a list of the problems with each student's courses.

1.

Owada, Miyako — **Grade 7** — **Student #003619**

Period/Course	Teacher	Room
1. Math 7	Delgado	33
2. PE/Health	Fields	Gym
3. Math 7	Chan	33
4. English 7	Wright	17
5. Science 7	Park	27
6. Band	Souza	Gym

2.

Kowalski, Charles M. — **Grade 7** — **Student #003606**

Period/Course	Teacher	Room
1. ESL 2	Reed	40
2. Spanish	Garcia	33
3. Math 7	Chan	10
4. ESL 1	Reed	Gym
5. PE/Health	Fields	27
6. Science 7	Park	

3.

Chan, Lori — **Grade 7** — **Student #003628**

Period/Course	Teacher	Room
1. Drama	Strasberg	11
2. Spanish	Garcia	40
3. Math 7	Chan	33
4. PE/Health	Fields	Gym
5. English 8	Wright	18

ACTING IT OUT.

Miyako, Chip, and Lori take turns telling Ms. Vasquez what is wrong with their schedules. Act out the conversations. Ms. Vasquez begins the conversation.

Would anyone like to sign up for one of our six-week mini-courses? They're something new we're trying this year. The mini-courses are offered after school.

KENNEDY AFTER-SCHOOL MINI-COURSE DESCRIPTIONS

Activity	Teacher	Grade Level
BABYSITTING: Do you want to earn extra money? Do you like children? This course will teach you how to take care of children.	Spock	7–8
MODEL ROCKETS: Construct and test-fly your own rocket! You'll order a model rocket from a catalog, then build and fly it!	von Braun	6–8
CULTURES AND CUISINE: Learn how to cook delicious dishes from different cultures around the world! You'll choose recipes and develop basic "survival skills" in the kitchen.	Waters	6–8
PHOTOGRAPHY: Shoot pictures, develop film, and print pictures in a darkroom!	Leibowitz	7–8

READING ABOUT IT.

Read the mini-course descriptions.

TALKING IT OVER.

Which Kennedy mini-course would you choose? Why?

WRITING AND SHARING.

Work with a partner. Design your own mini-course. Write a short description of your mini-course. Then share your course description with your classmates.

FINDING OUT. Work with classmates who have the same interest. Learn more about an after-school activity.

- ▲ When does the activity take place?
- ▲ Where does it meet?
- ▲ Who can participate.

Share what you've learned with your classmates.

LISTENING IN.

What kind of club is Miyako interested in? How about Zaida?

Ms. Reed: We also have lots of clubs. You might like to join a club.
Miyako: I'm interested in computers! Is there a computer club?
Ms. Reed: Yes. The Computer Club meets at 12:30 on Tuesdays and Thursdays.
Miyako: Do you want to join the Computer Club, Zaida?
Zaida: No. I already have a computer elective. What about photography? Is there a photography club? I love taking pictures.
Ms. Reed: I'm not sure. Let's check the Student Handbook.

READING ABOUT IT. Read about the clubs at Kennedy.

Clubs at Kennedy Middle School

Meet other students with the same interests! Join a club!

CLUB	MEETS
Languages and Cultures Club	The first Monday of the month after school in Ms. Reed's room.
Photography Club	Thursdays after school in room 40.
Computer Club	Tuesdays and Thursdays at 12:30 in room 36.
Drama Club	The last Friday of the month at 3:15 in room 34.
Science Fiction Club	Mondays at 3:30 in the library.
Science Club	Wednesdays after school in the science lab.
Nature Club	Every other Saturday morning in front of the school.

TUNING IN. Look at the list of Kennedy clubs again. Listen as Juan and Zaida discuss which club Juan is thinking about joining.

THINKING ABOUT IT. Give each club at Kennedy a clever name! Match each of these names with a club on the list.

a. The Ambassadors
b. The Mad Scientists
c. The Thespians
d. The Shutterbugs
e. The Backpackers
f. The Outer Space Cadets
g. The Hackers

LISTENING IN. What is Zaida taking pictures of?

Lori: So, you decided to join the Photography Club.
Zaida: Uh, huh.
Lori: What are you taking pictures of?
Zaida: Kids doing things. I'm taking shots of kids just being themselves. You know, candid shots.
Lori: Why?
Zaida: They're for the yearbook.

TALKING IT OVER.

Work with a partner. Look through Zaida's camera. Take turns describing what you see.

SHOW AND TELL. Bring in a favorite photo to share with your classmates. Tell who is in the photo, where the photo was taken, and what is happening. Answer any questions your classmates have about the photo.

UNIT 2

YOU MUST BE HOMESICK!

Ms. Vasquez: Lori, this is Michelle Marais. She's a new student at Kennedy. Lori will be your buddy, Michelle. She'll show you around and help you if you have any questions.

Lori: Hi, Michelle. Nice to meet you.

Michelle: Nice to meet you!

Lori: What grade are you in?

Michelle: Seventh.

Lori: Where are you from?

Michelle: Haïti.

Lori: Haïti! How long have you been here?

Michelle: Just two weeks.

Lori: Just two weeks? You must be homesick!

TUNING IN. Listen to the conversation. Then listen again and play the role of Michelle.

LISTENING IN. What is Michelle worried about?

Michelle: I'm more worried than homesick!
Lori: What are you worried about?
Michelle: Well, I'm worried about my teachers. And I'm worried about being late. I'm worried about homework . . . and I'm worried about . . .
Lori: Don't worry! Everybody worries about that stuff!

TALKING IT OVER. Here is a list of things that middle school students — especially new students — often worry about. Talk with a partner. Tell which things you worry about. Then add to the list.

WHAT I WORRY ABOUT . . .

Finding my classes	Getting an "F" on my report card
Being late	Changing in gym class
Having a mean teacher	Losing my lunch money
Getting into a fight	Being picked on
Having too much homework	Being laughed at
Forgetting my locker combination	Making new friends
Having something stolen from me	

THINKING ABOUT IT. Often an adult or a student can help you when you have a problem at school. Choose a situation from the list. Name someone who might help you solve the problem. For example, if you forgot your locker combination, who would you ask for help?

LISTENING IN.

What are Michelle and Lori looking at?

Michelle: I'm worried I'll get lost.
Lori: Here's a map of the campus. We're right here, near the counselor's office. Where's your homeroom?
Michelle: Room 31. Let's see . . . where is room 31?
Lori: Across the quad. You can't miss it. It's the fourth door from the end.

FIGURING IT OUT. Work with a partner. Name the places on the school map. Then think of other places on the map. Take turns describing and guessing those places.

1. It is to the west of the main building.
2. It is directly below room 22.
3. It is between room 9 and room 7.
4. It is behind the main office, off the foyer.
5. It is next to room 37.
6. It is opposite rooms 26 and 27, across the quad.
7. It is in front of the main building, near the main office.
8. It is directly above room 6.

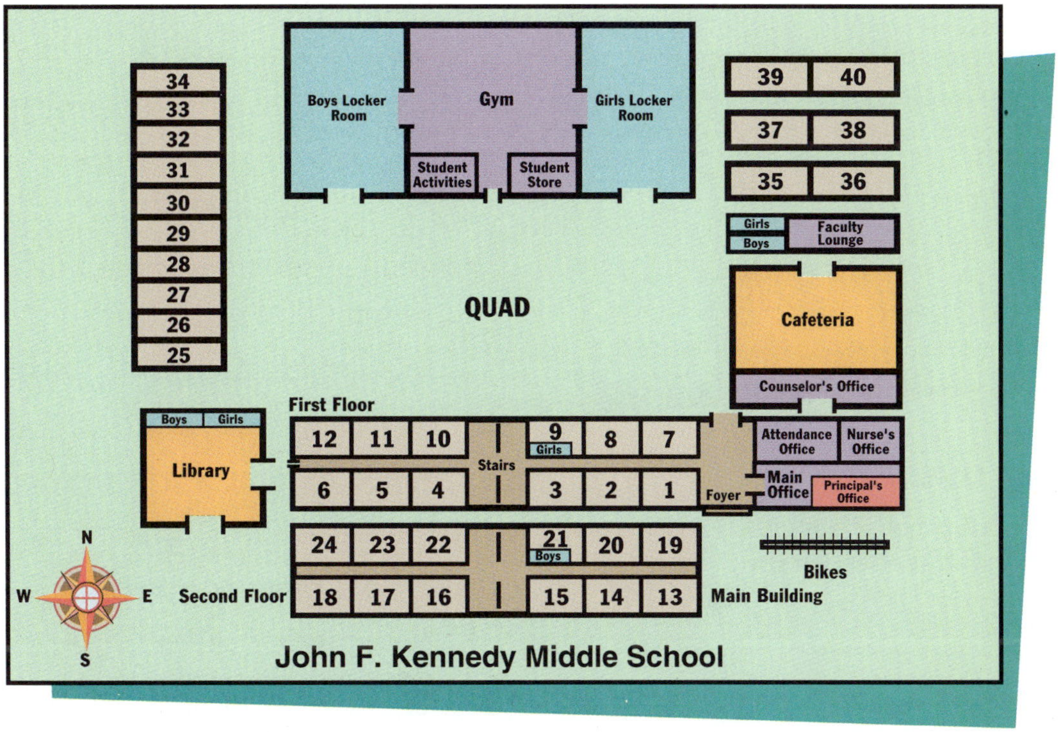

TUNING IN. Look at the school map. Listen to Lori and Michelle's conversation. Point to each place on the map that the girls are talking about.

LISTENING IN.

What does Michelle ask Lori for?

READING IT OVER.

Read the table of contents. Answer the questions about the Student Handbook.

Contents

1. On what page would you look to find out
   a. what time school starts?
   b. what to do if you lose your jacket?
   c. what to do if you have a doctor's appointment?
2. What part of the Handbook should you read if you want to
   a. ride your bicycle to school?
   b. take the school bus?
   c. know what you can buy with your Kennedy Cash?

TALKING IT OVER.

Read the school rules. Then give examples to explain each rule.

School Rules

Kennedy students are expected to . . .

1. be in the right place at the right time.
2. keep their hands and feet to themselves.
3. be courteous to others.
4. respect the rights and property of others.
5. cooperate with the adults on campus.
6. come to class ready to work.
7. be responsible for their own actions and remember the consequences.
8. use appropriate language with adults and other students.

FINDING OUT.

Work in groups of three. Read a section in your school's student handbook. Be ready to teach your classmates what the section tells you.

LISTENING IN.

What do teachers give students Kennedy Cash for?

Lori: If you follow the rules, you can earn Kennedy Cash.
Michelle: What's Kennedy Cash?
Lori: Teachers give it to you for good behavior. You can use Kennedy Cash to get discounts on things in the student store. You can also use it to buy things like pizza parties, lunchtime movies, and other special activities.
Michelle: Sounds great!

TALKING IT OVER.

How can a student earn Kennedy Cash? Read the list. Then give examples to explain each item. Is there anything you would add to the list?

You can earn Kennedy Cash by:

1. showing self-control.
2. obeying school and classroom rules.
3. not fighting.
4. being responsible.
5. taking pride in your school work.
6. being dependable.
7. showing good study habits.
8. completing work on time.
9. being quiet during free reading and study times.
10. showing good sportsmanship.
11. being cooperative.
12. showing self-respect.
13. being honest.

JUST FOR Fun

Kennedy Cash is a kind of reward system. Work in a small group. Design a reward system for your school or classroom. Think about these questions.

- ▲ What is the currency?
- ▲ How can you earn it?
- ▲ What special activities can you buy with it?
- ▲ How much does each special activity "cost"?

LISTENING IN. What is Michelle afraid of?

Michelle: I'm afraid that I won't make any friends!
Lori: Yes, you will!
Michelle: But how?
Lori: Just start up a conversation with someone. Introduce yourself. Make small talk.
Michelle: Small talk?
Lori: Yes. You know, say something that starts a conversation. Suppose you're sitting in class. You're waiting for the bell to ring . . .

ACTING IT OUT. Try this conversation with a partner. Play the roles of Michelle and Chip.

Practice making small talk. What else could Michelle say to start a conversation with Chip? What might Chip say back? Keep talking!

ACTING IT OUT. Make small talk with a classmate. Take turns starting a conversation in each of these situations. Use the conversation starters that are given, or think of other ways to begin.

A. You are standing in line in the cafeteria.

B. You are opening your locker.

C. You are browsing through new books in the library.

D. You are waiting for the school bus.

E. You are eating lunch outside.

F. You are standing on your number in gym class.

TUNING IN. Look at the pictures again. Listen to the conversation starters. Point to the situation or situations that match the words you hear.

FINDING OUT. Make a chart like this one. For each category, write your favorite and your least favorite thing. Then talk to your classmates. Find others who have the same likes and dislikes.

	My favorite	My least favorite
Radio station		
School subject		
Song		
Way to spend money		
Indoor activity		
Outdoor activity		
Thing to do with a friend		
Place to go shopping		
TV show		
Food		

JUST FOR Fun

Look in your locker or at home for something that is very important to you. Bring the item to class. Tell your classmates why it is important. What does the item say about you?

WRITING AND SHARING. Work in small groups. Think of questions you might ask to get acquainted with someone. Make a chart. Then share it with other groups.

WHAT? What is your favorite food?	WHO? Who is your favorite singer?
WHERE? Where do you live?	WHEN? When is our next day off?

TUNING IN. Listen to the questions. After each question, write down your answer.

LISTENING IN. What are the students playing this semester?

Michelle: It's almost 8:15. It's time for homeroom. I'd better go.
Lori: I'm in Mr. Chavez's homeroom. Whose homeroom are you in?
Michelle: Ms. Reed's.
Lori: Hey, we're playing you today after school!
Michelle: Playing us?
Lori: Yes, in the Super Class Competition. Every Wednesday after school our homerooms compete against each other.
Michelle: Compete against each other?
Lori: For the Super Class Award at each grade level. Sometimes we compete in a sport. This semester we're playing Trivia.
Michelle: Trivia?
Lori: We're late. Here . . . read about it in *The Fun Times*. Why don't you come? You'll have a good time, and you'll meet other kids.

READING ABOUT IT.

Read more about the Super Class Competition.

FINDING OUT.

Getting involved in clubs and other activities is a good way to make new friends. Work with a partner. Make a list of clubs and activities at your school. Then share the information with your classmates.

The Fun Times

Activities Bulletin for Kennedy Middle School • Fall Edition

SUPER CLASS COMPETITION

Homerooms to Compete This Fall in Trivia Tournament

Kennedy students will play Trivia this fall in the school's Super Class Competition. The winning homeroom at each grade level will earn the title Super Class. Each Super Class will compete in Kennedy's schoolwide Triple Dare Assembly at the end of the semester.

Trivia is a popular game that tests players' knowledge of the world around them.

The games will be held every Wednesday after school in Ms. Reed's homeroom. Each homeroom will select a player to represent the class.

FIGURING IT OUT. When you play Trivia you ask questions that match the answers on the game board. Work in a small group. Ask as many questions as you can. For example: On the gameboard you read: Babe Ruth played this sport. You ask: What is baseball?

U.S. Presidents	Team Sports	Geography	Money	U.S. National Holidays
This person is living in the White House today.	A team has five players on the court.	California borders this ocean.	His picture is on a penny.	We celebrate President's Day in this month.
He is called the father of his country.	The players wear helmets and shoulder pads.	This country is also a continent.	His picture is on a dime.	We remember the pilgrims on this day.
He was president during the Civil War.	Babe Ruth played this sport.	This mountain is the highest in the world.	His picture is on a twenty dollar bill.	We honor American workers on this day.
$800	The players use pucks and sticks.	This river is the longest in the world.	His picture is on a one hundred dollar bill.	$800
$1,000	$1,000	$1,000	His picture is on a silver dollar.	$1,000

LISTENING IN.

Why is Shelley moving to another city?

Shelley: That was fun! I don't know your name. My name's Shelley.
Michelle: I'm Michelle. Michelle Marais. I just moved here.
Shelley: And I'm moving away next week to another city.
Michelle: Moving away? Why?
Shelley: My mother got a new job.
Michelle: That's too bad! I thought we could be friends!

TUNING IN. Listen to the rest of the conversation between Shelley and Michelle. As you listen, take notes. Then answer these questions. What does Michelle miss about her old school? What does she like about her new school?

ON YOUR OWN. A journal is a place to write your private observations, thoughts, ideas, and feelings. Start keeping a journal.

- Use a notebook or a special composition book with blank pages.
- Leave wide margins on each page. This will give you space to add comments when you later reread your writing.
- Write down anything that comes to mind. Describe an event, jot down an interesting quote, or write about a person. Remember that only you will read what you write.
- Your journal can serve as a source for future writing ideas in school. Make your journal entries as lively and detailed as possible.
- Try to write each day. You'll learn more about yourself and the world around you.

THINKING ABOUT IT. Have you ever changed schools? If so, what do you miss about your old school? What do you like about your new school? Begin your journal by answering these questions.

UNIT 3

WHY DON'T YOU SLEEP OVER?

Chip: Here's a picture of my family.
Juan: Wow! Six brothers!
Chip: Yeah, and one bathroom.
Juan: It must be a lot of fun around here.
Chip: I have an idea! Why don't you sleep over? There's no school tomorrow.
Juan: Shouldn't you ask your mother?
Chip: She won't mind.
Juan: OK! But I have to call my uncle.

TUNING IN.

Look at the photo. Listen as Chip tells Juan about each of his brothers. Point to the boy that Chip is talking about.

FIGURING IT OUT. Ask and answer these questions about Chip's family. Then think of other questions to ask.

- ▲ How is Michael Kowalski related to Chip?
- ▲ How is Zev Kowalski related to Chip?
- ▲ How are Matthew and Jane O'Leary related to Chip?
- ▲ Who are Chip's cousins?
- ▲ Who are Chip's uncles?

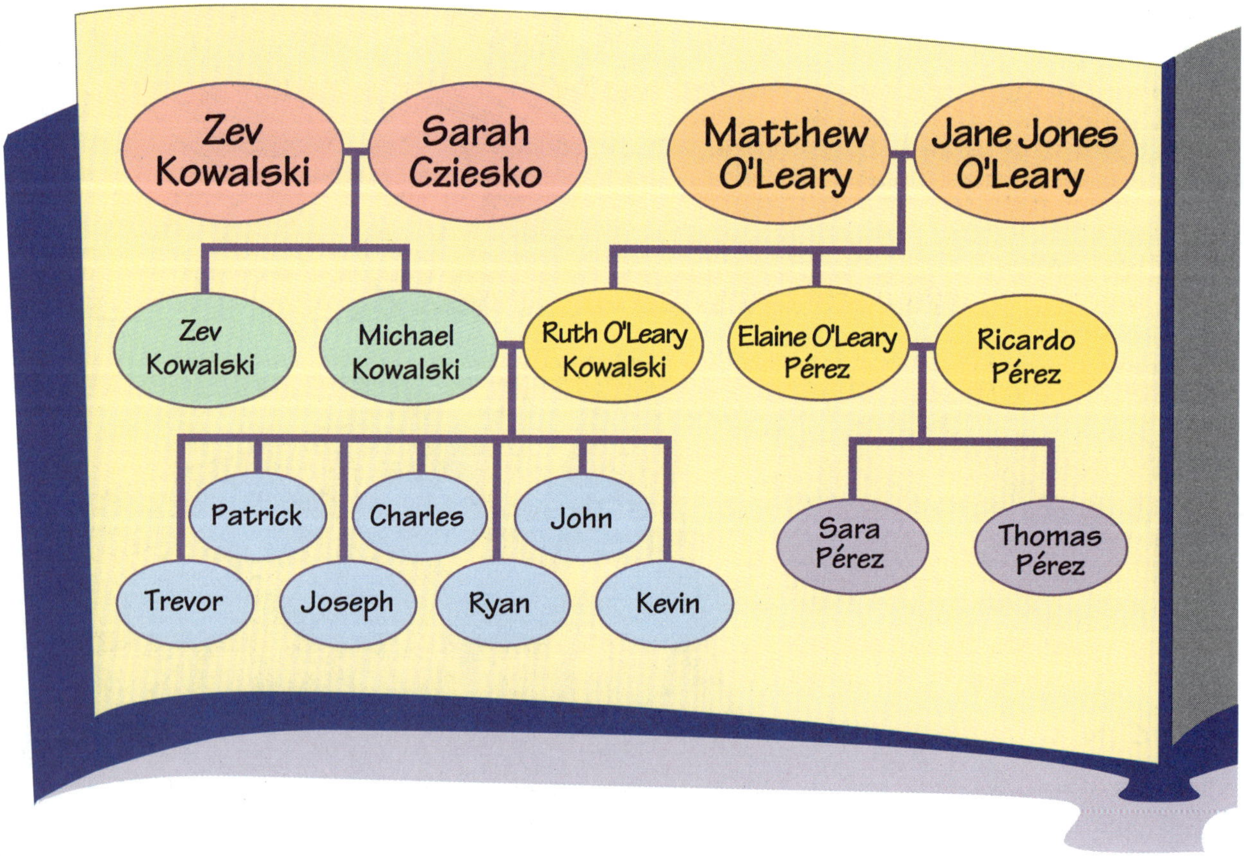

ON YOUR OWN. Draw your family tree. Put as many branches on the tree as you can. Then share your family tree with your classmates.

TUNING IN. Look at the photos of Chip's relatives. Listen as Chip tells Juan about the people in them. Point to the photo that Chip is talking about.

THINKING ABOUT IT. Imagine that Juan is being introduced to each person in Chip's family tree — including Chip's brothers. How would Juan say hello to each person?

LISTENING IN. Who is Juan going to meet at dinner?

TALKING IT OVER. Name and describe your family members.

THINKING ABOUT IT.

What would your family members say about you? Make a chart. Use the words in the box. Add other words, too!

boring	immature	nice
carefree	interesting	obnoxious
friendly	kind	relaxed
funny	lazy	selfish
generous	loving	stubborn
hard-working	mature	sincere
responsible	easygoing	talkative

TUNING IN. You are going to hear a list of words that describe people. Point your thumb up if the word is a compliment. Point your thumb down if the word is a criticism. Point your thumb sideways if you are not sure!

FIGURING IT OUT. Read the clues about the Kowalski brothers. Name each person and point to him in the photo.

1. He is older than Chip but younger than Trevor and Patrick.
2. He is younger than Chip but older than John.
3. He is younger than John.
4. He is the same age as Trevor!
5. He is the oldest child in the family.
6. He is the youngest child in the family.
7. He is younger than Joe but older than Ryan.
8. They are the same age because they are twins.

TUNING IN. Listen to the Kowalskis at dinner. Everyone needs something he or she cannot reach. Point your thumb up if the person asks politely. Point your thumb down if he or she asks impolitely.

TALKING IT OVER. Look at the picture. Answer the questions.

1. Who is sitting at the ends of the table?
2. Who is sitting between Patrick and Juan?
3. Who is sitting on Mrs. Kowalski's left?
4. Where is Ryan sitting?
5. Where is Chip sitting?
6. Where is Trevor sitting?

FIGURING IT OUT. Work with a partner. Read the information and draw a picture to show where each person in the Kowalski family usually sits.

The Kowalski family almost always eats dinner together. Each person usually sits in the same place. Mr. and Mrs. Kowalski usually sit at opposite ends of the table. Kevin sits on Mrs. Kowalski's right, and Patrick sits on her left. Chip sits on Mr. Kowalski's right, and John sits on his left. Trevor sits between Chip and Patrick. Joe sits between Kevin and Ryan. Chip and Ryan never sit next to each other because they fight too much! But tonight the Kowalski's have a guest! Not everyone is sitting in his or her usual place.

JUST FOR Fun

Work in groups of three or four. What do you think the Kowalskis talk about at the dinner table? Write a short conversation. Then act it out.

TALKING IT OVER.

It is usually Joe's job to set the table, but tonight Joe is not home. Tell Chip how to set the table. Answer his questions.

1. Where does the plate go?
2. Where does the dinner fork go?
3. Where does the knife go?
4. Where does the spoon go?
5. Where does the salad fork go?
6. Where does the water glass go?
7. Where does the napkin go?

ACTING IT OUT.

You are a dinner guest at the Kowalski's house. What do you need? Don't be shy. Ask!

1.

2.
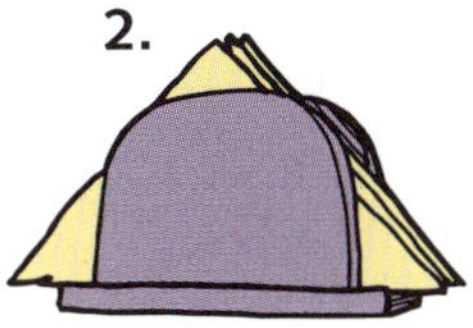

3.

4.

5.

6.
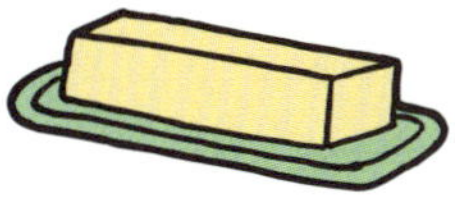

7.

8.

9.

10.

11.

LISTENING IN. What does Chip's mother tell him to do?

FIGURING IT OUT.

Name the items in Chip's bedroom.

alarm clock	lamp	chest of drawers
desk	bookshelf	pillow
blanket	mattress	clock radio
dresser	bunk bed	sheet
blinds	mirror	

JUST FOR Fun

Work with a partner. Take turns describing your bedroom or the room you sleep in. As you describe the room, your partner will draw it.

- ▲ How well did you describe your room?
- ▲ How well did your partner draw what you described?

ACTING IT OUT. Help Chip clean his room. Tell him where to put each item that is in the wrong place.

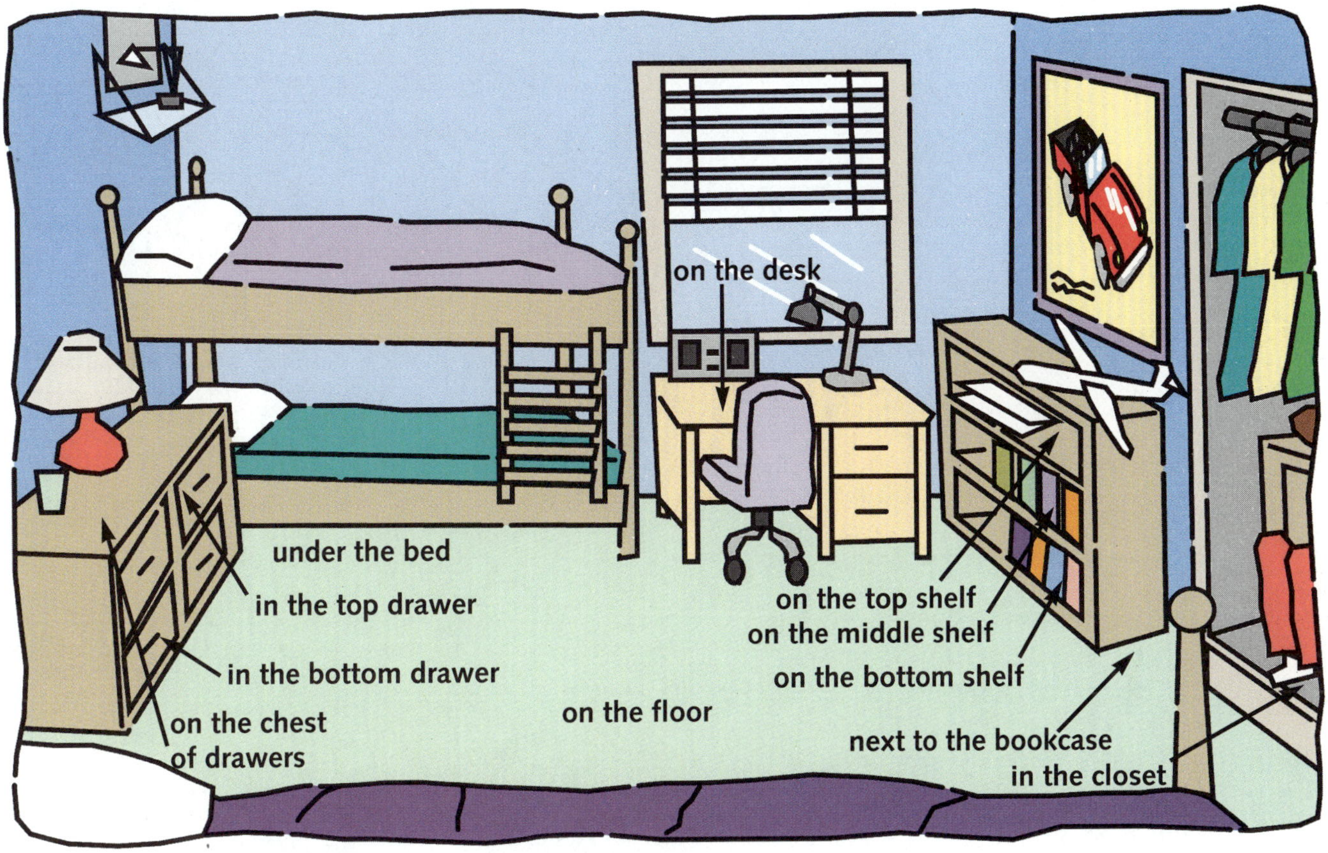

ON YOUR OWN.

Make a list of your ten most important personal possessions. Tell where you keep each item.

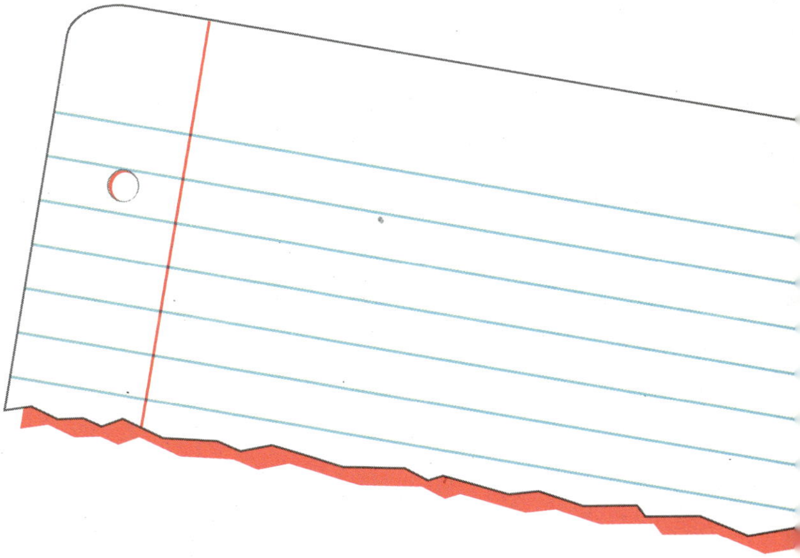

LISTENING IN. Who does Chip share a bedroom with?

Chip: This is my bed. The lower bunk is Trevor's. The upper bunk is mine. The other two bunks are Patrick's and Joe's.
Juan: Whose hockey stick is that?
Chip: It belongs to Trevor. He likes hockey.
Juan: What about the football helmet?
Chip: That's Patrick's. He's good at football. He plays for Washington High.
Juan: Are those his trophies?
Chip: No, those are Joe's. He won them for Washington High in the Academic Decathlon.

WRITING AND SHARING.

Do you share a room with another member of your family? What things are yours? What things are not yours? What things do you share? Make a chart. Then share your chart with your classmates.

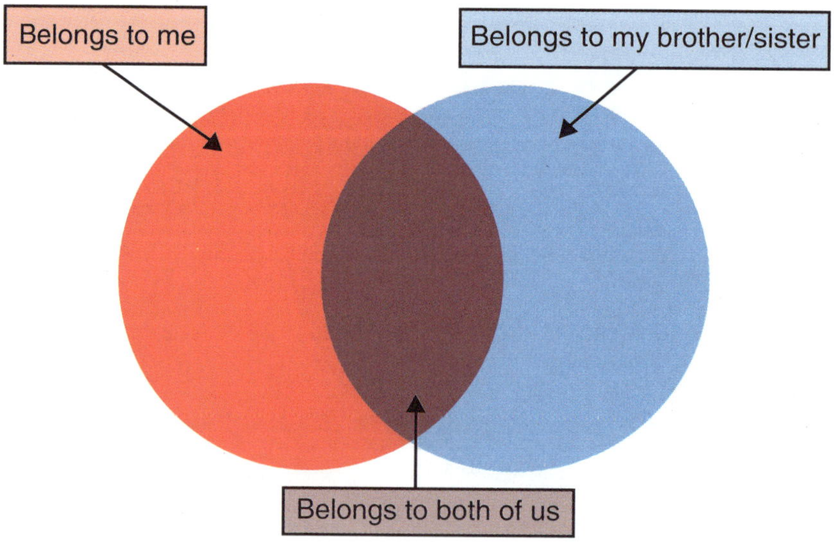

LISTENING IN.

What does Patrick tell Chip to do?

Patrick: Hey, are you wearing my pullover?
Chip: It's not your pullover! It's Trevor's.
Patrick: Well, put away your clothes. This room's a mess!
Chip: These aren't my clothes! They're yours!
Patrick: Mine? They're not mine! They're yours . . . or Joe's.

ACTING IT OUT.

Pretend that you are Chip. Tell Patrick who each item belongs to.

long-sleeved shirt

loafers

short-sleeved shirt

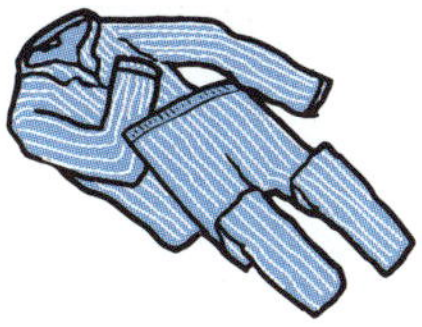
pajamas

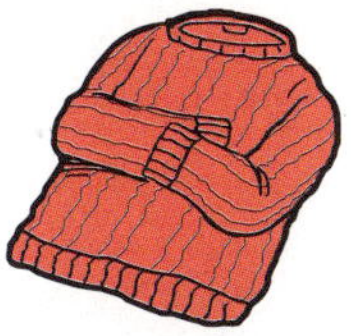
pullover

shorts

flannel shirt

undershirt

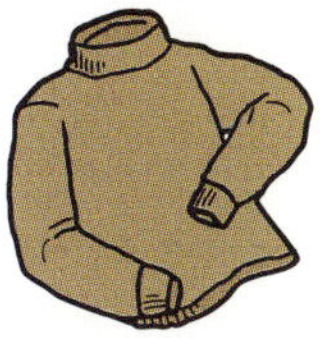
turtleneck

bathrobe

jeans

running shoes

pants

hiking boots

sports coat

baseball cap

running shorts

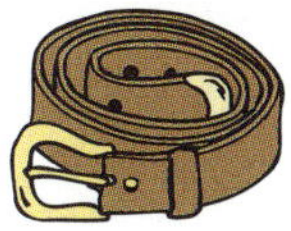
belt

ON YOUR OWN. Make a picture dictionary that shows the clothes and other items in your closet. Label each item.

LISTENING IN.

Where are Juan and Chip going?

Chip: Trevor! Hurry up in there!
Trevor: Hold your horses!
Chip: Juan and I have a baseball game this morning.
Trevor: I'll be out in a minute.
Chip: Open up! We all have to share the bathroom!
Trevor: Ouch! I cut myself!
Chip: You cut yourself?
Juan: How did he cut himself?
Chip: He's probably practicing shaving again!

TUNING IN.

Listen in as Trevor practices shaving. Act out Trevor's words.

FIGURING IT OUT.

The Kowalski family has just one bathroom. Help the family make a bathroom schedule for a typical weekday. Make a chart like this one and fill in the times.

	GET UP	EAT BREAKFAST	USE BATHROOM
Mrs. Kowalski			
Mr. Kowalski			
Trevor			
Patrick			
Joe			
Chip			
Ryan			
John			
Kevin			

UNIT 4

LET'S CHECK OUT THE EXHIBITS!

Lori: Wow! Look at all the display tables!

Michelle: What should we look at first?

Lori: What do you want to know more about?

Michelle: Just about everything! I'd really like to know what causes acne.

Lori: And I'd like to know more about why smoking is bad for you.

Michelle: I'd like to know more about why it's important to eat right. I wonder . . . is junk food always bad for you?

Lori: I want to know more about how to take good care of my teeth.

Michelle: Me, too. Let's check out the exhibits!

TUNING IN. Listen to each statement. For each health issue the girls mention, point your thumb up if you would like to know more about it, too.

Health Assessment

1. I do not smoke.
2. I do not use alcohol or other drugs.
3. I avoid fatty foods.
4. I avoid eating too much sugar.
5. I get enough sleep.
6. I exercise at least three times a week.
7. I brush my teeth at least twice a day.
8. I have a medical checkup once a year.
9. I see the dentist every six months.
10. I have my eyes checked every two years.

FIGURING IT OUT.

Match each statement with the correct picture.

a. 

b. 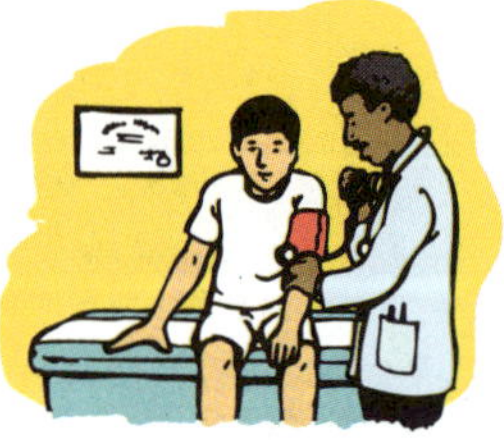

c. 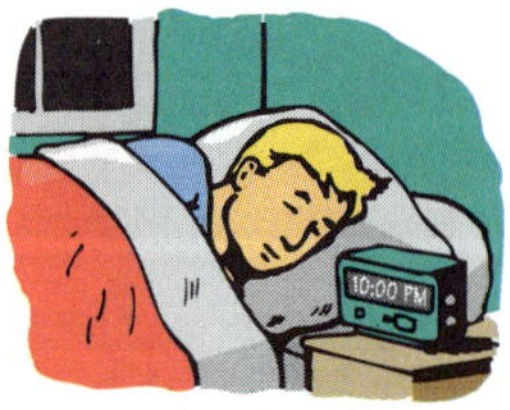

d. 

e. 

f. 

g. 

h. 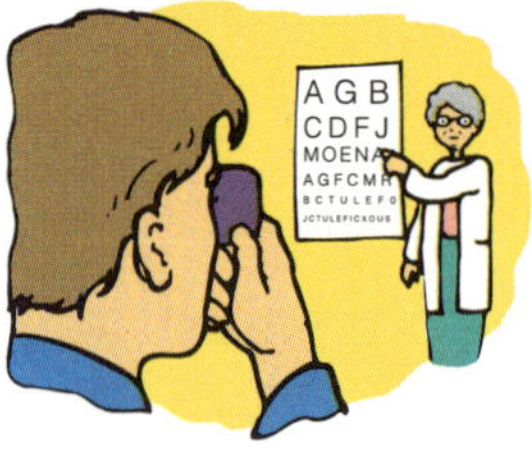

i. 

j. 

TUNING IN. Listen as Lori reads the computerized health assessment. For each statement, point your thumb up if your answer is "yes." Point your thumb down if your answer is "no."

LISTENING IN.

Why does Lori tell Michelle that her weight is "just about right"?

Lori: How much do you weigh?
Michelle: I can't believe it! I weigh 120 pounds! I'm way too heavy!
Lori: No, you're not. Look at the chart. How tall are you?
Michelle: Five feet four. That's 64 inches.
Lori: You have a medium build. Your weight is just about right.

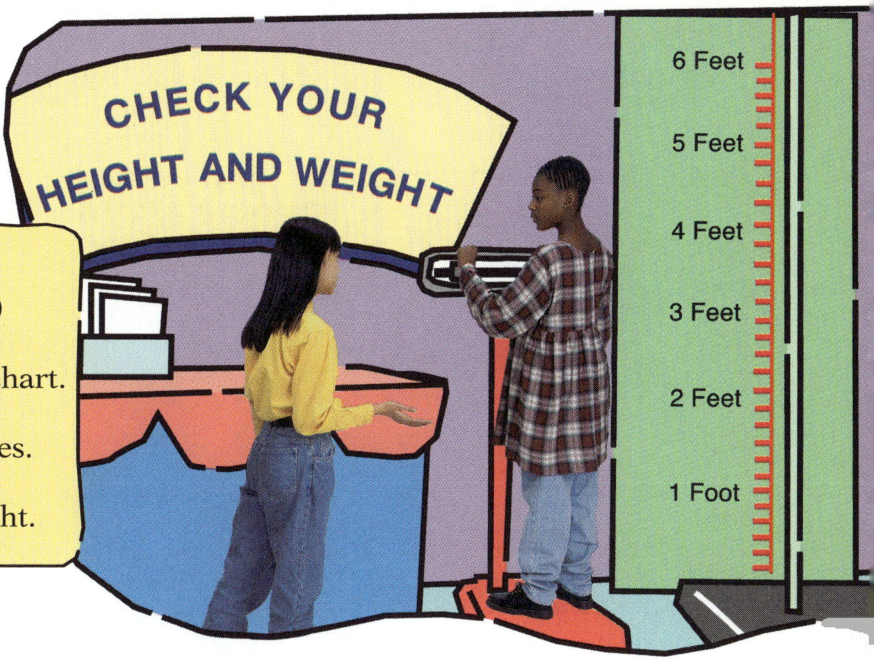

AVERAGE WEIGHT FOR HEIGHT TABLE

GIRLS 11-15

HEIGHT (INCHES)	AGE (YEARS) 11	12	13	14	15
50	61	62			
51	63	65			
52	65	67			
53	68	69	71		
54	71	71	73		
55	74	75	77	78	
56	78	79	81	83	
57	82	82	84	88	92
58	86	86	88	93	96
59	90	90	92	96	100
60	95	95	97	101	105
61	99	100	101	105	105
62	104	105	106	109	113
63		110	110	112	116
64		114	115	117	119
65		118	120	121	122
66			124	124	125
67			128	130	131
68			131	133	135
69				135	137
70				136	138
71				138	140

BOYS 11-15

HEIGHT (INCHES)	AGE (YEARS) 11	12	13	14	15
50	58	58			
51	61	61			
52	64	64	64		
53	67	68	68		
54	70	71	71	72	
55	73	74	74	74	
56	77	77	78	78	80
57	81	81	82	83	83
58	84	85	85	86	87
59	88	89	89	90	90
60	92	92	93	94	95
61	95	96	97	99	100
62	100	101	102	103	104
63	105	106	107	108	110
64		109	111	113	115
65		114	117	118	120
66			119	122	125
67			124	128	130
68				134	134
69				137	139
70				143	144
71				148	150
72					153
73					157
74					160

FIGURING IT OUT.

Describe each boy or girl. Use the charts.

Ziang
Age 12
5′3″
105 pounds

James
Age 13
5′6″
145 pounds

Carlos
Age 15
5′5″
123 pounds

Alex
Age 14
5′6″
98 pounds

Carmen
Age 11
5′1″
92 pounds

LISTENING IN. Does what you eat affect how you look?

TALKING IT OVER.

Name some of the problems that an unhealthy diet or poor eating habits can cause. Discuss them with your classmates.

TUNING IN.

Lori and Michelle each want a snack. What will they eat? Listen as they try to decide. Point your thumb up if the food item is healthy. Point your thumb down if it is not healthy.

fast food

cupcakes

oatmeal cookies

candy

ice cream

fresh fruit

potato chips

caramel corn

milk

raw vegetables

Choosing a healthy diet

1. Eat less fat.
2. Eat more fiber: whole grains, fruits, and vegetables.
3. Eat less sugar.

TALKING IT OVER.

What can you do to improve your diet?

ACTING IT OUT.

Pretend that you just ate your favorite snack. What did you eat? Tell your classmates.

I ate an apple.

I had a few carrot sticks.

I drank some milk.

I had several oatmeal cookies.

I had a little ice cream.

LISTENING IN. Do you think Dr. Johnson does a good job explaining how people get cavities?

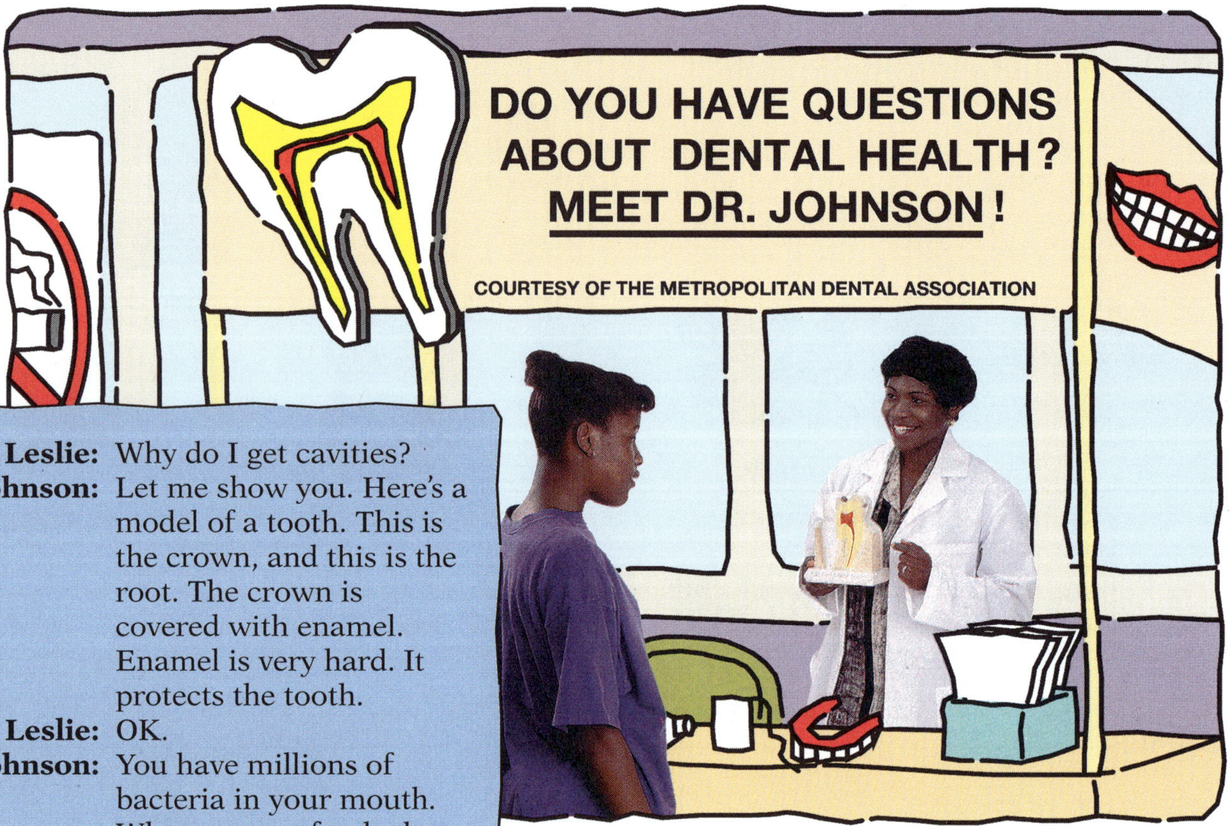

Leslie: Why do I get cavities?

Dr. Johnson: Let me show you. Here's a model of a tooth. This is the crown, and this is the root. The crown is covered with enamel. Enamel is very hard. It protects the tooth.

Leslie: OK.

Dr. Johnson: You have millions of bacteria in your mouth. When you eat foods that contain sugar . . .

Leslie: Like candy bars . . .

Dr. Johnson: Exactly . . . the bacteria produce acids that eat through the enamel. The bacteria then get inside the tooth and cause the tooth to decay.

Leslie: And that's how a cavity starts to form, right?

Dr. Johnson: Right. Unless a dentist cleans out the cavity and fills the hole, the decay will spread down into the root. The tooth could die.

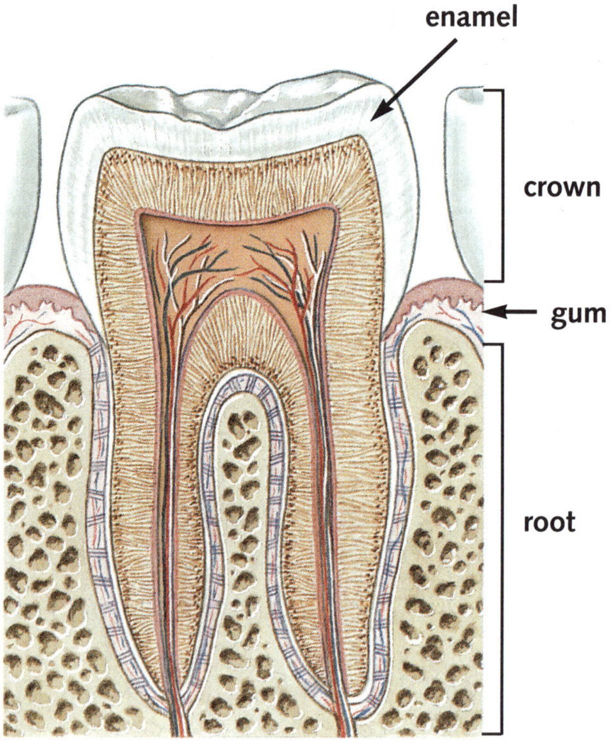

ON YOUR OWN.

Illustrate Dr. Johnson's words. Make a poster that shows how a cavity forms.

LISTENING IN.

What does Dr. Johnson tell Leslie about flossing?

TUNING IN.

Listen as Dr. Johnson tells Leslie how to floss and brush her teeth. Act out Dr. Johnson's words.

READING ABOUT IT.

Read this page from the brochure and the dental health tips.

FLOSS EACH DAY... STOP TOOTH DECAY

1. First break off about eight to ten inches of floss. Wind the floss around your middle fingers. Use your thumbs to hold it tight.

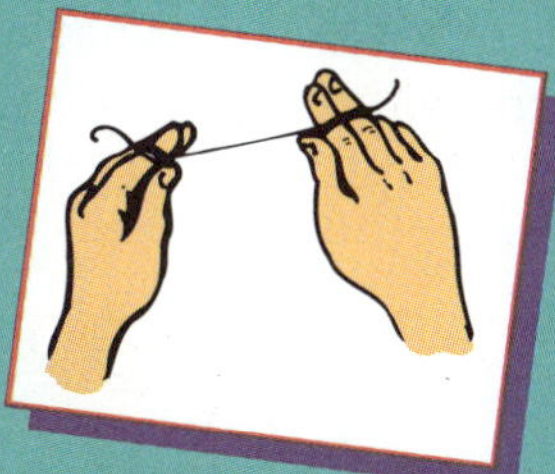

2. Work the floss between each pair of teeth. Be gentle. Move the floss back and forth. Then move it up and down against each tooth.

3. Now it's time to brush. Place the brush at an angle against your gums and teeth. Move the brush in a circle. Brush all of your teeth.

Dental Health Tips

- Eat healthy food. Avoid sugar.
- Floss daily.
- Brush after every meal and before going to bed.
- Use a toothpaste with fluoride.
- Use a toothbrush. Be sure to reach all the surfaces of each tooth and your gums.
- Visit your dentist twice a year. See your dentist immediately if you have a problem.

TALKING IT OVER.

Work with a partner. First read the two statements. Then discuss the questions. Take notes about your ideas as you talk. Be ready to share your ideas with your classmates.

- Tooth decay is one of the most common diseases today.
- More than half the U.S. population did not visit a dentist last year.

1. Why do so many people fail to take good care of their teeth?
2. Why do so many people avoid seeing the dentist?

ON YOUR OWN. Make a list of foods that could cause tooth decay.

LISTENING IN. What words do Lori and Michelle use to describe cigarettes?

Lori: Look . . . here's a display about smoking. I think cigarettes are disgusting!

Michelle: They're gross! Smoking can make you look sick. Look, here's a brochure on smoking.

JUST FOR Fun

Work with a partner. Make a poster that shows what happens to you when you smoke. Share your poster with your classmates.

TUNING IN. Listen to the statements about smoking. If you believe a statement is true, point your thumb up. If you believe a statement is false, point your thumb down.

READING ABOUT IT.

Read this page from the brochure.

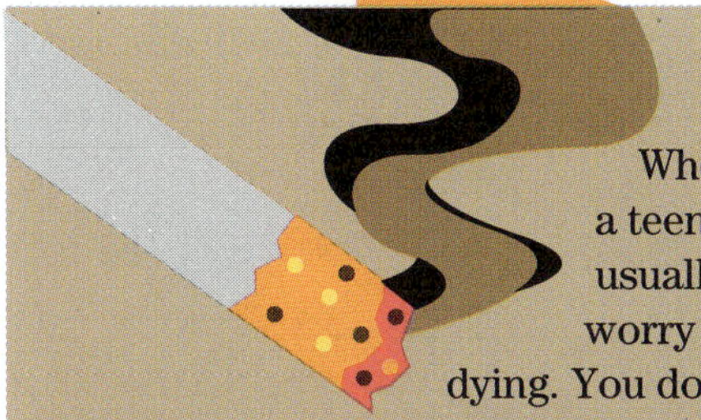

When you're a teenager, you usually don't worry about dying. You don't worry about illnesses such as lung cancer and heart disease. But you should!

Smoking causes nearly 400,000 deaths a year. A burning cigarette contains 4,000 chemical substances—50 of which can cause cancer! Eighty percent of all lung cancer deaths are related to smoking. Smokers have twice as many heart attacks as nonsmokers. In fact, doctors think that every cigarette a person smokes cuts six minutes from his or her life.

The good news is that fewer and fewer teenagers are deciding to smoke.

STARTING YOUNG: Teenage Smoking

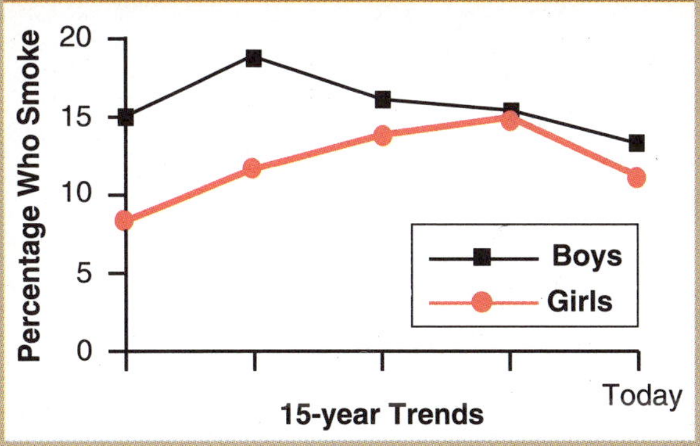

FIGURING IT OUT.

What does the line graph in the brochure tell the reader? Explain the graph in your own words.

WRITING AND SHARING.

Make a list of reasons why smoking is harmful. Then share your list with your classmates.

FINDING OUT.

Find out how much a pack of cigarettes costs. Then figure out how much money someone who smokes a pack a day spends in a year — just on cigarettes!

READING ABOUT IT.

Read the information in the display.

Lakeside Medical Center
Your Life Is in Our Hands

When to Call the Doctor: Warning Signs

- A cough that lasts more than three weeks
- Temperature higher than 102° or temperature over 100° that lasts more than a week
- Continued vomiting or diarrhea
- Ear discomfort
- Hoarseness that lasts more than a week
- Extreme weakness in one part of the body
- Fainting or severe dizziness
- A headache that lasts more than one day
- Abdominal pain lasting more than three hours
- Swollen glands with sore throat and fever
- Any severe pain that doesn't go away within a short time
- Sudden weight loss

LISTENING IN. Why does Michelle think that she is coming down with a cold?

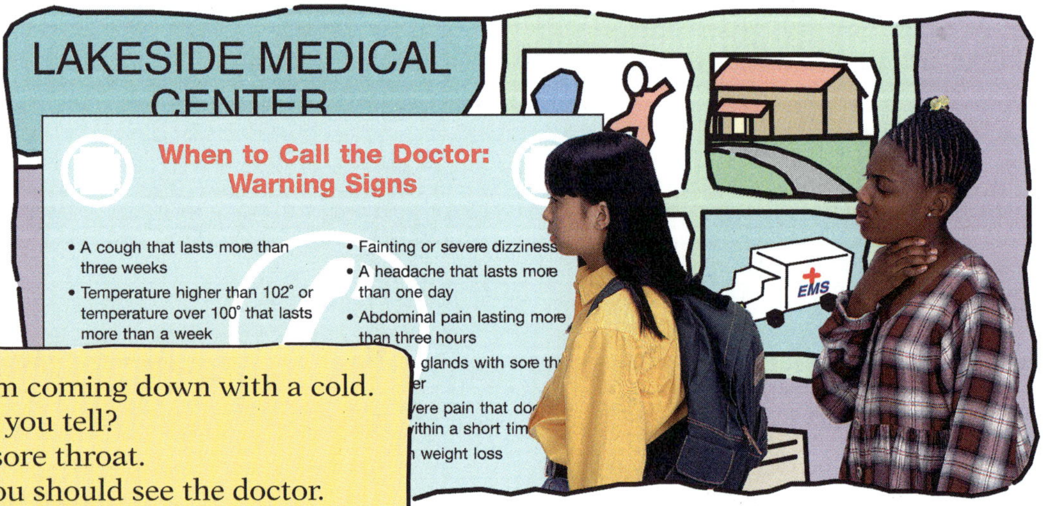

Michelle: I think I'm coming down with a cold.
Lori: How can you tell?
Michelle: I have a sore throat.
Lori: Maybe you should see the doctor.
Michelle: Oh, I don't think so.
Lori: Maybe you should ask the school nurse for advice.

ACTING IT OUT. Pretend that you have the symptoms of a health problem. Ask the school nurse for advice.

FIGURING IT OUT. Match the over-the-counter medicines or products to the health problems or symptoms.

1. a sore throat
2. the flu
3. a rash
4. a cut
5. a cold
6. a cough
7. a headache
8. runny nose

a. aspirin

b. cough syrup

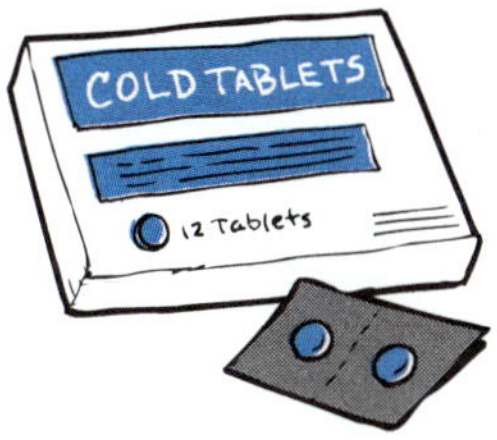

c. cold tablets

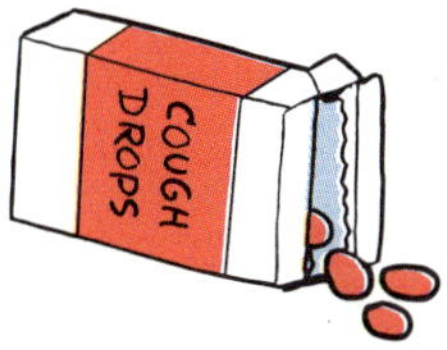

d. cough drops

e. throat lozenges

f. nasal spray

g. ointment

h. Band-Aids

THINKING ABOUT IT.

Read the label before you take any medicine! Ask yourself the following questions.

1. What is this medicine for?
2. How much or how many should I take?
3. How should I take it?
4. Are there any possible side effects?

Answer these four questions for this label.

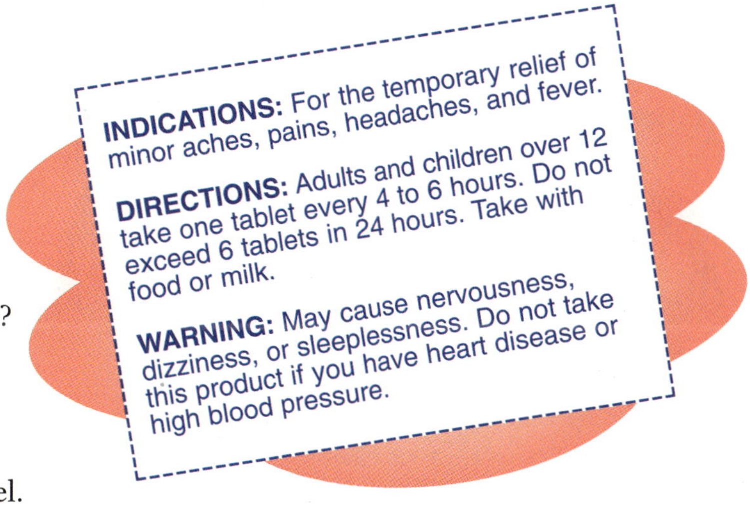

FIGURING IT OUT.

Match each prize to the organization or group you think donated it.

PRIZES

a. Illustrated medical dictionary
b. Crate of apples
c. Gift basket of dried fruit
d. Running shoes
e. Aerobics video
f. "Cooking with Cottage Cheese" video
g. Baseball cap
h. Weights
i. Goggles
j. Gift certificate for camping equipment

DONORS

1. Metropolitan Dairy Association
2. The Great Outdoors
3. Books Unlimited
4. Mariner Swim Club
5. Metropolitan Little League
6. Sunrise Health Spa
7. Lakeshore Organic Grocery
8. In a Nut Shell
9. Pumping Iron Gym
10. Cobbler's Footwear

TUNING IN. Listen as Mr. Fields thanks each donor. How many prizes did you match with the correct donor?

THINKING ABOUT IT. Mr. Fields is about to draw for the prizes. What prize is each of these students hoping for?

Zaida likes jogging.

Chip likes baseball.

Lori likes healthy food.

Juan likes hiking.

John likes working out.

UNIT 5

COULD YOU LEND ME SOME MONEY?

Chip: Juan! What's the date today?
Juan: November 6. Why?
Chip: The sixth? Oh, no! My dad's birthday is tomorrow! I almost forgot!
Juan: How old is he?
Chip: I don't know . . . really old! You're not supposed to ask.
Juan: Are you going to give him a gift?
Chip: Yes. Will you help me pick one out?
Juan: Sure. Let's try the mall. We'll find something there.
Chip: Good idea. By the way, could you lend me some money? I'll pay you back.

TUNING IN. Chip can't decide what to buy his dad. Listen as Juan makes some suggestions. For each one, point your thumb up if you think it's a good suggestion. Point your thumb down if you think it's a bad suggestion.

LISTENING IN.

Has Chip borrowed money from Juan before?

Juan: Lend you money? Again?
Chip: My allowance isn't enough! My parents only give me fifteen dollars a week!
Juan: Fifteen dollars? That's plenty! You get more than I do. I only get ten!
Chip: Please, Juan! I'll pay you back next week. I promise.
Juan: How much do you want to borrow?
Chip: Fifteen dollars.
Juan: That's too much. You can borrow five.
Chip: Ten.
Juan: OK. Ten. But you have to pay me back right away.

TALKING IT OVER.

Do you agree with Juan? Is Chip's allowance enough? How much money do you think a middle school student needs each week?

- more than enough
- plenty
- not enough
- too little

THINKING ABOUT IT. Work with a partner. Help Chip, Juan Lori, and Michelle spend their allowances. Don't forget to stay within their budgets.

LISTENING IN.

What does Chip say his dad needs?

Chip: So, anyway, what should I buy my Dad?
Juan: What does he need?
Chip: Well, he needs new socks. His socks all have holes in the toes!
Juan: That's not a very exciting gift. What does he want?
Chip: I have no idea!
Juan: How about a tie?

WRITING AND SHARING. Suggest items that Chip might buy his dad. Decide whether the item is a "need" or a "want." Make a chart. Be ready to share your ideas with your classmates.

Needs	Wants

TALKING IT OVER. What things do you spend your money on that you really need? What things do you spend money on that you do not need, but just want?

JUST FOR Fun

Imagine that you win a contest. The prize is one hundred dollars. Describe what you would do with the money. Would you save it? Would you spend it? What would you spend it on?

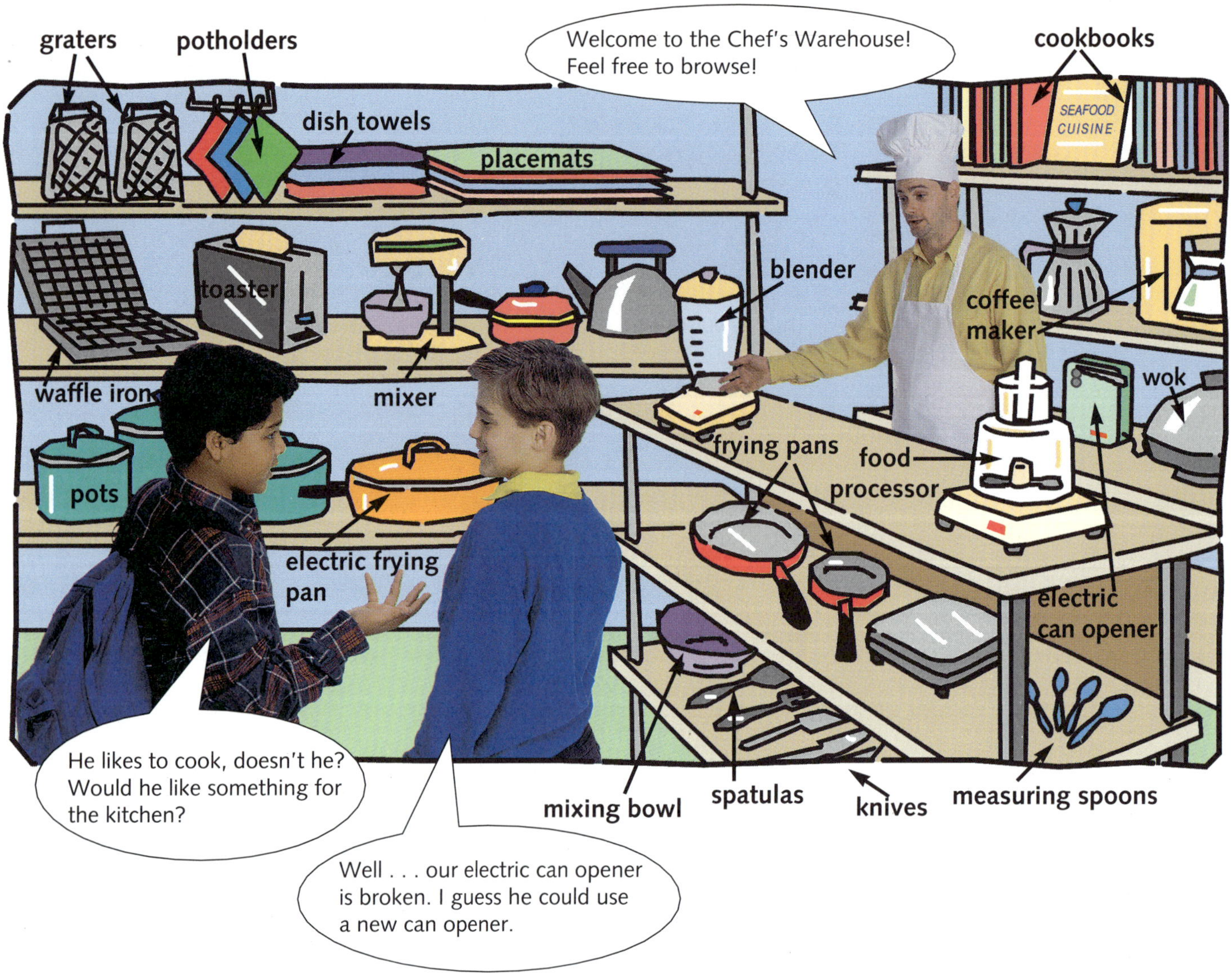

THINKING ABOUT IT. Think about these questions.

- ▲ Which items at this store do you think would make good gifts? Why?
- ▲ Who would like the gift?
- ▲ Is there something at this store that you would like for yourself?

Compare your ideas with your classmates.

TALKING IT OVER.

Talk with a partner. Name the items you have in your home. Describe where each item is kept.

LISTENING IN.

Do you think Chip and his dad like the same kinds of music?

JUST FOR Fun

Make a list of recording artists — singers, musicians, or groups — that an adult in your family likes. Then make a list of your own favorites. Compare and discuss your lists with a partner.

TUNING IN. Listen to some music selections. Write the word or phrase you think describes each piece.

LISTENING IN. What does Chip decide to get his dad?

Chip: I think I'll get him a shirt.
Juan: That's a safe bet.

Sales clerk: May I help you?
Chip: I'm looking for a shirt.
Sales clerk: How much do you want to spend?
Chip: Under twenty-five dollars.
Sales clerk: Most of our shirts are more than twenty-five dollars. Let's check the sale table. All the shirts on the sale table are marked down 30 percent.

ACTING IT OUT. With a partner, play the roles of Chip and Juan. Help Chip choose a shirt. Which shirts are the least expensive?

this one	this blue one
that one	that red one
these	these blue ones
those	those red ones

JUST FOR Fun

You receive a gift certificate for one hundred dollars. How would you spend the money at your favorite clothing store?

TALKING IT OVER. Work with a partner. Tell which shirts you like and which you don't like. Use gestures as well as words.

ACTING IT OUT.

Imagine that you are shopping with a friend who just can't decide. You are becoming impatient. What will you say?

THINKING ABOUT IT. You want to buy a gift for a family member. You are thinking of buying an item of clothing. Choose the family member and make a list of what he or she needs.

LISTENING IN. What size shirt does Chip's dad wear?

Sales clerk: What size shirt does he wear?
Chip: I'm not sure!
Sales clerk: Well, how tall is he?
Chip: He's about five ten.
Sales clerk: How much does he weigh?
Chip: About 160.
Sales clerk: Then he probably takes a shirt with a 33" sleeve and a 15" neck. I'd say he wears a medium. This shirt is too small.
Chip: But I love this shirt!

ON YOUR OWN. Imagine that you could choose the ideal outfit for an adult in your family. How would that person be dressed? Write a detailed description.

- ▲ Think of details that will help create a vivid picture. Choose your words carefully.
- ▲ How will you organize your description? Describe the person from head to toe. Begin with the details that would first catch someone's attention or that are the most important.
- ▲ Have a classmate read your description. Do your words create a vivid and entertaining snapshot? Is your description interesting and fun to read?

My grandmother is very active, and she really likes to have fun. I am going to describe what she is wearing for her 75th birthday party. She has on a lovely black hat. I call it a garden hat because it has a bunch of purple, red, and yellow flowers on the top, and there's a bright orange silk butterfly sitting on the rim. She has a long purple scarf around her neck. It floats behind her like wings when she walks! Her fire engine-red silk jacket and purple skirt really make her stand out in a crowd! To complete the outfit, she is wearing black leggings and shiny new cowboy boots.

TUNING IN. Listen to the conversation. Do you agree or disagree with the sales clerk's advice?

LISTENING IN. Why does Chip tell Juan to find something else?

Juan: Chip, you'd better find another one. That one is way too small!
Chip: But I like this one!
Juan: There are lots of others on the sale table. Choose something else!
Chip: But I don't see any others I like.
Juan: I'm telling you . . . the one you're holding won't fit him. You'll be sorry.

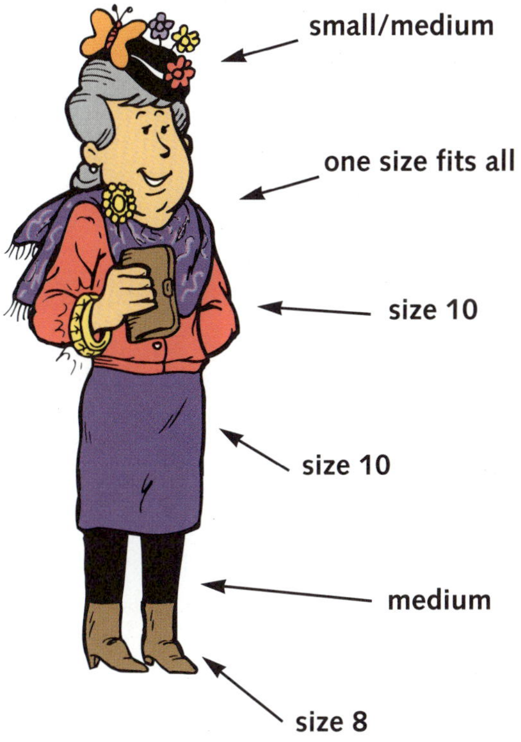

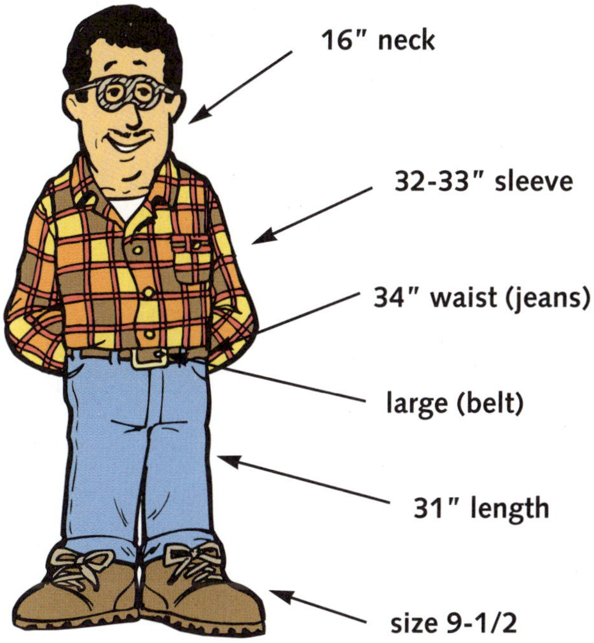

FINDING OUT. What clothing sizes do the members of your family wear? Guess, then check!

LISTENING IN.

Does Chip decide to buy the Hawaiian shirt?

Chip: I still like this shirt! I'm going to take a chance. I'll take it! How much is it?
Sales clerk: Let's see. It's regularly twenty-eight dollars. It's marked down 30 percent.
Chip: So it should be about twenty dollars, right?

FIGURING IT OUT.

Complete the chart. Estimate the sale price of each item.

ITEM	REGULAR PRICE	MARK DOWN	SALE PRICE: YOUR ESTIMATE
shirt	$24.00	30% off	______
shoes	$49.95	25% off	______
underwear	3 pairs for $12.00	20% off	______
parka	$65.00	40% off	______
sweater	$29.00	1/2 price	______
belt	$22.00	15% off	______
bathrobe	$67.50	1/3 off	______

ESTIMATING.

Estimating is something you do every day. Estimating is an important math skill — and an important life skill!

When you go shopping, you estimate whether you have enough money to buy something. When your teacher gives you a homework assignment, you estimate how long it will take you to do it. Think of other examples of estimating. Share your examples with classmates.

ESTIMATING AND CHECKING.

Practice estimating. Read the questions. For each one, first write your estimate — your best, most careful guess. Then check your estimate.

- ▲ How many times do you blink your eyes in a minute? Have someone keep time and count for you.
- ▲ How many cups of coffee does the average adult drink in a day? Ask at least ten people.
- ▲ How many fives are there in the numbers between one and one hundred? Can you figure this out in your head?
- ▲ How many tables are there in the school cafeteria? Count the tables in one row. Then count the number of rows and multiply.
- ▲ How many times do you open your locker in a week? Keep a tally in your locker.

LISTENING IN.

How much is the sales tax on clothing where you live?

Sales clerk: That's $19.60. With tax, it comes to $20.78!
Chip: How much is tax?
Sales clerk: It's 6 percent.
Chip: Here's $21.00.
Sales clerk: Thank you! That's $20.78, .79, .80, .90 and $21.00.
Chip: Thank you!

TUNING IN. Listen to some transactions between Chip and a sales clerk. For each transaction, write down the amount of money Chip should get back from the sales clerk.

FIGURING IT OUT. Estimate the total amount of each sale below, including sales tax. Then check each estimate. How close did you come to the exact price?

Amount	+ 4% sales tax	Total	+ 5% sales tax	Total	+ 6% sales tax	Total
$100.00						
$60.00						
$10.00						
$14.50						
$25.00						

ACTING IT OUT. Work with a partner. One of you will play the clerk, and the other will play the customer. Act out each transaction. The sales tax is 6 percent.

SINGING ALONG. Does someone in your class have a birthday today? Sing happy birthday to your classmate.

ACTING IT OUT.

Pretend that you are Mr. Kowalski. Thank the people who have given you gifts. Use the words in the box.

too short	too tight
too long	too baggy
too small	not large enough
too big	not long enough
too large	not small enough

JUST FOR Fun

Is there a birthday song in your own language? Teach your classmates the words and the tune.

ON YOUR OWN.

Your grandparents have sent you an item of clothing as a gift, but you just can't wear it — especially not to school! Write them a thank you letter. What will you say?

UNIT 6

I WONDER WHAT THEY WOULD SAY ABOUT US!

Ms. Goldstein: I'd like you to imagine that it's the year 3000. A team of anthropologists is hunting through the ruins of Kennedy Middle School. They wonder about life here. They wonder about what we were like.

Juan: Wow! I wonder what they would say about us!

Ms. Goldstein: The team finds a time capsule. It's filled with artifacts, or objects, that show what life was like at Kennedy a thousand years earlier.

Juan: Cool.

Ms. Goldstein: Let's make a time capsule. We can use this plastic storage bin. I want everyone to contribute something.

Neelam: Like what?

Ms. Goldstein: Think about it. Each of you should choose an object that tells something about the students here at Kennedy.

TUNING IN. Listen as Juan and Tran discuss what they might put in the time capsule. Then suggest some objects that would tell something about the students at your school.

LISTENING IN. What does Ms. Goldstein say a culture is? If you can, add to her definition.

Ms. Goldstein: What an interesting variety of objects! They reveal something about the different cultures represented here at Kennedy, don't they?

Juan: Ms. Goldstein, what's a culture?

Ms. Goldstein: *Culture* is a word used to describe people's way of life. People who share the same culture share the same way of life. They share the same language. They share many of the same beliefs. They often live in the same place, eat the same types of food, and have the same customs, or ways of doing things.

THINKING ABOUT IT. If possible, work with a partner who speaks the same first language as you do. Make a chart. List the ways you are alike. List the ways you are different. Do you share the same culture? Talk about why or why not.

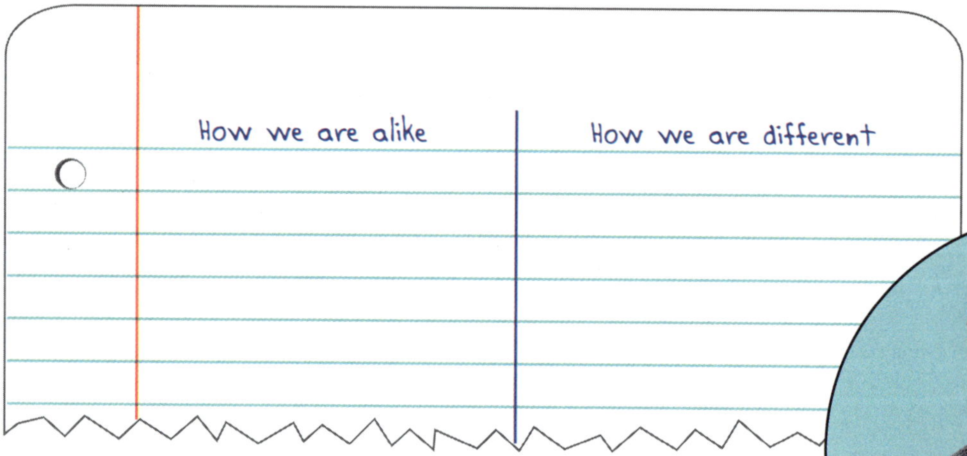

TALKING IT OVER. Can people change cultures? Do you think people can belong to more than one culture? Talk with your classmates.

TUNING IN. Everyone belongs to many different groups. Listen as some Kennedy students talk about themselves. For each group a student mentions, point your thumb up if you are a member of that group. Point your thumb down if you are not a member of it.

TALKING IT OVER. Here are some of the artifacts that Ms. Goldstein's students placed in the time capsule. What do these artifacts reveal about Kennedy's many cultures? Discuss with your classmates.

1.

2.

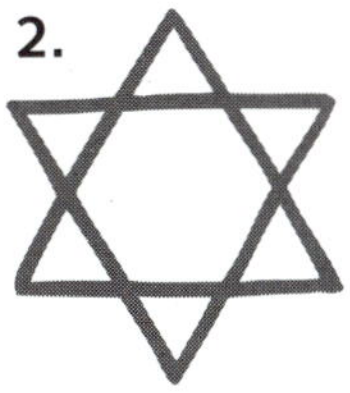

3.

4.

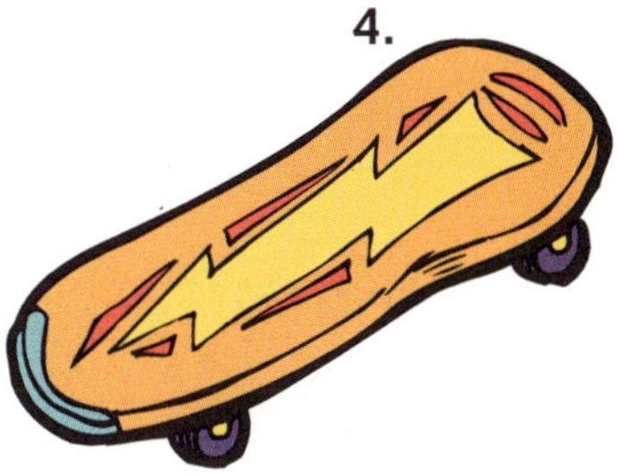

5.

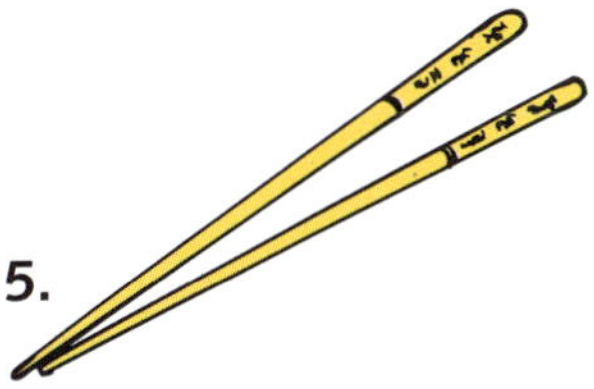

6.

7.

8.

9.

10.

11.

12.

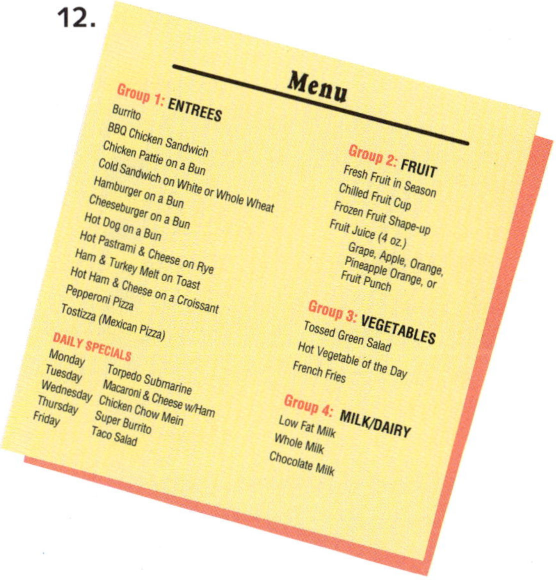

Menu

Group 1: ENTREES
Burrito
BBQ Chicken Sandwich
Chicken Pattie on a Bun
Cold Sandwich on White or Whole Wheat
Hamburger on a Bun
Cheeseburger on a Bun
Hot Dog on a Bun
Hot Pastrami & Cheese on Rye
Ham & Turkey Melt on Toast
Hot Ham & Cheese on a Croissant
Pepperoni Pizza
Tostizza (Mexican Pizza)

DAILY SPECIALS

Monday	Torpedo Submarine
Tuesday	Macaroni & Cheese w/Ham
Wednesday	Chicken Chow Mein
Thursday	Super Burrito
Friday	Taco Salad

Group 2: FRUIT
Fresh Fruit in Season
Chilled Fruit Cup
Frozen Fruit Shape-up
Fruit Juice (4 oz.)
Grape, Apple, Orange, Pineapple Orange, or Fruit Punch

Group 3: VEGETABLES
Tossed Green Salad
Hot Vegetable of the Day
French Fries

Group 4: MILK/DAIRY
Low Fat Milk
Whole Milk
Chocolate Milk

13.

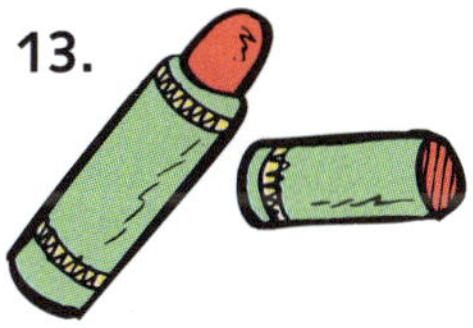

14.

LISTENING IN. Why is the Kennedy student body changing?

TALKING IT OVER. Which nationalities are represented in your classroom?

FINDING OUT. Match each flag to the nationality.

a. 
b. 
c. 
d. 
e. 
f. 
g. 
h. 
i. 
j. 
k. 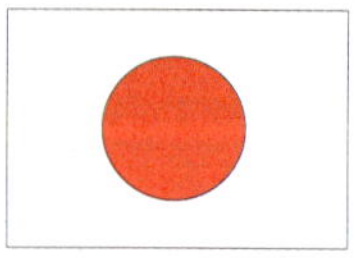
l. 
m. 
n. 
o. 
p. 
q. 
r. 
s. 
t. 

1. Brazilian
2. Cambodian
3. Chinese
4. Colombian
5. Cuban
6. Dominican
7. Filipino
8. Guatemalan
9. Haitian
10. Honduran
11. Italian
12. Japanese
13. Korean (South)
14. Laotian
15. Mexican
16. Nicaraguan
17. Puerto Rican
18. Romanian
19. Russian
20. Taiwanese
21. Thai
22. Ukranian
23. Vietnamese

u. 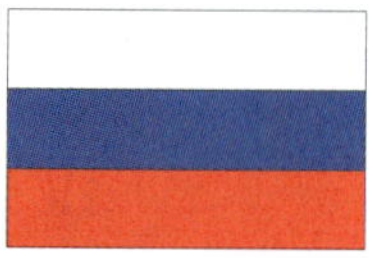
v. 
w. 

WRITING AND SHARING. Work with a partner. Make a list of reasons why people come to the United States from other countries. Be ready to share the list with your classmates.

TUNING IN. Review the map and carefully read the information about the new immigrants to the United States. Then listen to the statements about the map. Point your thumb up if a statement is true. Point your thumb down if it is false.

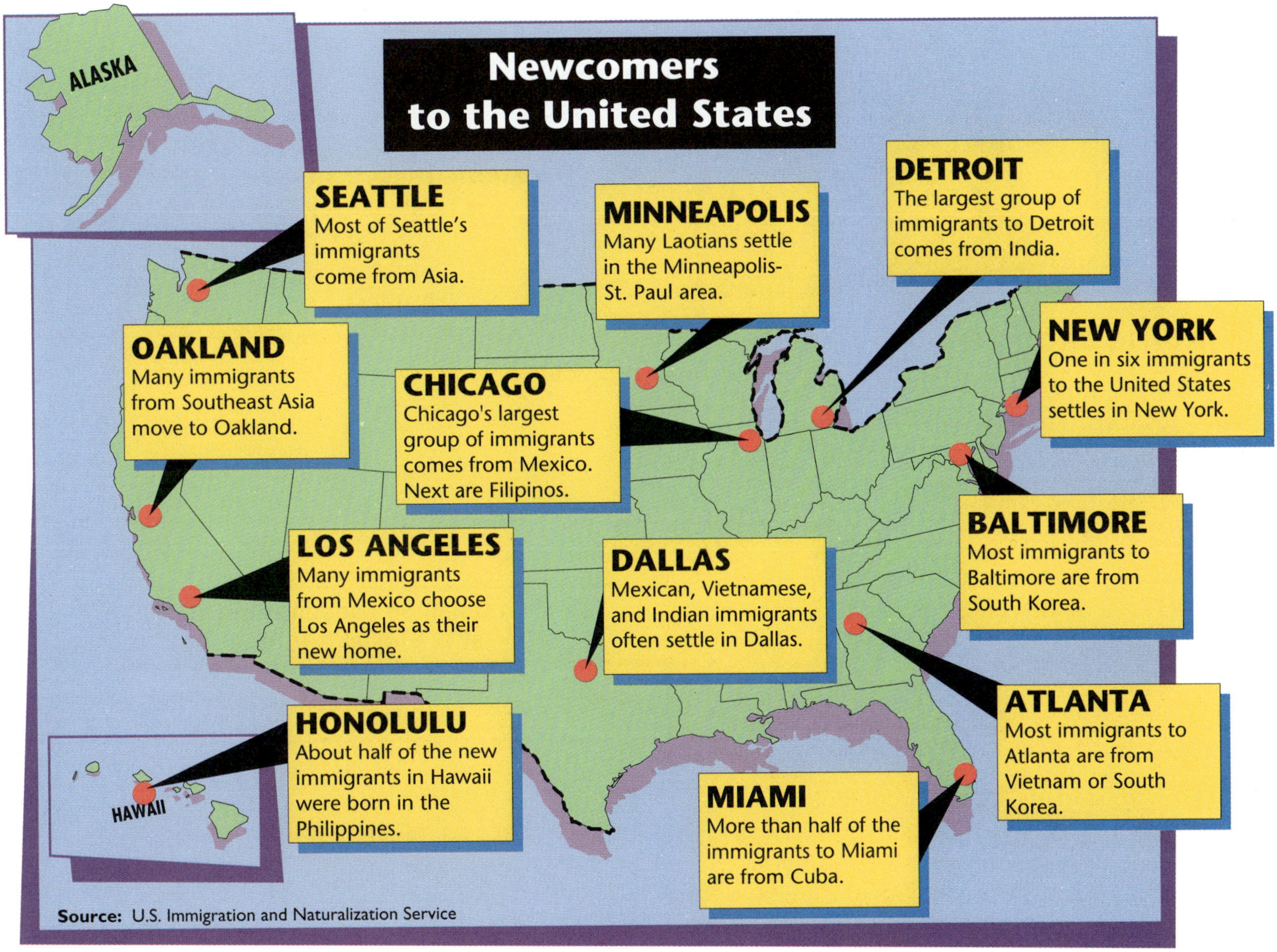

TALKING IT OVER. Talk with your classmates. Think about your own communities. Describe their ethnic makeup.

Most people are . . .	About one in five is . . .
Many people are . . .	About a third are . . .
A few are . . .	About half are . . .

LISTENING IN. What first language do many of the Kennedy students speak?

Ms. Goldstein: More and more students at Kennedy speak a first language other than English.

Juan: Right! Lots of kids speak Spanish.

Neelam: And a few speak languages like Tagalog, Arabic, and Cantonese!

Ms. Goldstein: In fact, a national census is taken every ten years. The U.S. government gathers data on languages spoken in U.S. homes.

READING ABOUT IT.

Use the reading and the chart to answer the questions. Then ask and answer other questions with your classmates.

1. In 1990, how many people spoke Korean at home?
2. Did the number of Chinese speakers decrease or increase between 1980 and 1990?
3. The number of speakers of which language increased the most between 1980 and 1990?

The U.S. Census Bureau reported in 1990 that 31.8 million Americans speak languages other than English at home, up from 23.1 million ten years earlier.

After English, Spanish is the most common language in U.S. homes. The number of Spanish speakers has increased by 50 percent since 1980.

Ten Most Common Languages in the U.S. after English — 1990

Language	Number of Speakers in 1990	Percentage Change from 1980
Spanish	17.3 million	50%
French	1.7 million	8%
German	1.5 million	-4%
Italian	1.3 million	-20%
Chinese	1.2 million	98%
Tagalog	840,000	87%
Polish	723,000	-12%
Korean	626,000	127%
Vietnamese	507,000	150%
Portuguese	430,000	19%

Source: Bureau of the Census, U.S. Department of Commerce, 1990

TUNING IN. Look at the chart and listen to the statements about it. Point your thumb up if a statement is true. Point your thumb down if it is false.

FINDING OUT. What languages other than English are spoken at your school? Try to find out (or make good estimates) how many students speak each language. Make a pie chart that summarizes the data.

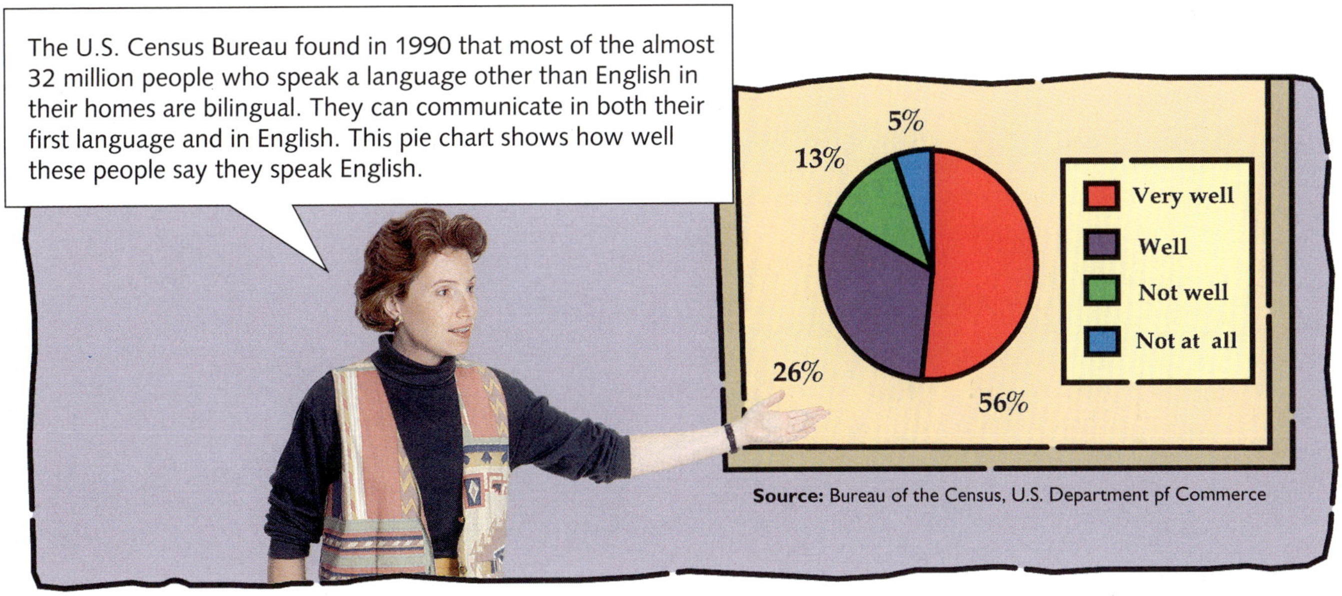

FINDING OUT.

How well do you and your classmates speak English? Make a class chart. Put your name in the appropriate column.

Speaks English very well	Speaks English well	Does not speak English well	Does not speak English at all

TALKING IT OVER. Work in small groups. Discuss these questions.

- ▲ What language(s) do you speak at home?
- ▲ Who in your family is bilingual?
- ▲ Are there members of your family who don't speak any English?
- ▲ Who speaks better English in your family — the adults or the children?

THINKING ABOUT IT. Some people seem to learn a second (or even a third!) language more quickly than other people. What characteristics do "good" second-language acquirers have? Continue the list. Discuss your list with your classmates.

A good language learner is someone who is not
1. shy.
2. afraid of making mistakes.

LISTENING IN. What kinds of things do people from different cultures borrow from each other?

FIGURING IT OUT. The words on Ms. Goldstein's board are from Native American languages. Can you figure out the words in English that we use today?

THINKING ABOUT IT. Work in a group of three or four. Make a chart that shows things that have been borrowed from different cultures by the "majority" U.S. culture. Add as many cultures as you would like to the chart.

	Borrowed from the Latino culture	Borrowed from the Chinese culture	Borrowed from the ________ culture
Food			
Customs			
Everyday Words			
Other			

JUST FOR Fun

People in many different cultures throughout the world eat bread. Make a collage or a poster that shows breads from different parts of the world. Label each kind of bread.

ACTING IT OUT.

Tell what you will bring to the potluck lunch. Bring something that is not already on the table.

TUNING IN. You are at a potluck dinner! Listen to each request. Point your thumb up if the food asked for is a thing you can count. Point your thumb down if it is a thing you can't count.

LISTENING IN.

What is body language?

Ms. Goldstein: When people from different cultures come in contact, they sometimes have a hard time understanding each other.

Neelam: Because they don't speak the same language?

Ms. Goldstein: It's not just a matter of words. For example, I can tell you're from another country. And it's not just your accent!

Neelam: What else?

Ms. Goldstein: It's your body language.

Neelam: Body language?

Ms. Goldstein: Right. What you do with your hands. The look on your face. The way you stand.

Neelam: Really?

ACTING IT OUT. What kinds of body language do you use? Show your classmates

1. how you say "Yes."
2. how you say "No."
3. how you say "Speak up!"
4. how you say "Be quiet!"
5. how close you stand to a good friend.
6. how close you stand to your teacher.
7. how you say "I like you!"
8. how you tell others you're happy.
9. how you tell others you're sad.
10. how you sit at home.
11. how you sit at school.

TALKING IT OVER. Do you know what it means when someone . . .

snaps her fingers?

winks at someone?

blows on his fingernails and then rubs them on his chest?

ACTING IT OUT. Show how speakers of English communicate without words. Use body language!

I know! I don't know!

I'm interested in this! I'm bored!

That's good! That's bad!

Come here! Stay away!

It's over here! It's over there!

JUST FOR Fun

Work with a partner. Draw examples of body language you think is rude or annoying.

LISTENING IN.

What are some ways you can stereotype someone?

Neelam: Ms. Goldstein, it seems like we have some problems here at Kennedy.
Ms. Goldstein: Say more about that . . .
Neelam: You know. Some kids hang around only with kids of their own race.
Juan: And sometimes there are fights.
Ms. Goldstein: Unfortunately, you're right. Prejudice is a problem. Stereotyping is a problem.
Juan: What's stereotyping?
Ms. Goldstein: That's when we assume that all people of a certain group are the same.
Tomás: Like sneaky, or stupid, or greedy.
Ms. Goldstein: Right.

TALKING IT OVER.

Work with two or three classmates who share the same cultural background. Discuss how people sometimes stereotype others. Keep track of your discussion on a chart. Share your chart with others.

- ▲ Do you sometimes judge people just because they are different than you are?
- ▲ What are some of the stereotypes people might have about you?
- ▲ Do you ever stereotype others?

How people sometimes stereotype me	How I sometimes stereotype others

WRITING AND SHARING.

Work with a partner. Discuss steps that could be taken to reduce prejudice in your school or community. Make a list of positive ideas. Then share your ideas with your classmates.

UNIT 7

I WANT TO BE A BETTER STUDENT!

Ms. Goldstein:	I've asked you to stay after school, Tomás, because I'm worried about your work. You're getting D's.
Tomás:	That's because the book is so boring!
Ms. Goldstein:	That's only an excuse. You're capable of much better work.
Tomás:	But I always come to class.
Ms. Goldstein:	That's not enough. You need to listen. You need to take good notes. And you need to do your homework.
Tomás:	But I do my homework!
Ms. Goldstein:	Well . . . let's take a look at this study skills questionnaire.

STUDY SKILLS QUESTIONNAIRE

	rarely	sometimes	often	always
1. I have a quiet place to study at home.	1	2	3	4
2. I have a time each day when I do my homework.	1	2	3	4
3. I look at clues in my textbook such as headings, pictures, and the captions under pictures. I also look carefully at tables and diagrams.	1	2	3	4
4. When I study, I ask myself, "Does this make sense? Do I understand what I'm reading?"	1	2	3	4
5. I ask my teacher for help when I don't understand something.	1	2	3	4
6. When there's a test coming up, I start studying right away.	1	2	3	4
7. I use my notes and homework to get ready for a test.	1	2	3	4
8. I try to think of questions that might be on the test.	1	2	3	4

TUNING IN.

Look at the questionnaire. Listen as Ms. Goldstein reads each entry. Then listen again and answer each entry by circling the number you think applies to you. Write the number of your response.

LISTENING IN. Does Tomás think he needs help?

WRITING AND SHARING. What else do good students do? Work with a partner. List your ideas. Then share them with your classmates.

THINKING ABOUT IT. Which classes are you doing well in? What are the reasons for your success? Make a chart.

I'm doing well in . . .	because . . .

TUNING IN.

Listen to the reasons that students give for doing well in their classes. Point your thumb up if the reason has to do with good study habits.

JUST FOR Fun

Make a report card for yourself. Rate your own study skills. First list five abilities that you think are important for success in school. Then give yourself a grade for each ability or skill.

GIVING DIRECTIONS.

Giving directions is also an important skill. When you give directions, follow these steps.

1. Tell your listeners the purpose of your directions.
2. Give the directions one step at a time. Make sure the steps are in the right order.
3. Be clear. Give all the information the listeners need.
4. Check to see if your listeners understood your directions. Ask questions to make sure they understand.

Now try it! Think of something you know how to do or make.

- ▲ Write out the directions. Make sure the steps are in the right order. Use words from the box.
- ▲ Give the directions to your classmates. Make sure you include all the important details.
- ▲ Check for understanding! Ask questions.

first	next
second	now
third	last
then	finally

TUNING IN.

Listen to Ms. Goldstein. Follow her directions. Point to the picture that matches each step for making American Indian fried bread.

a.
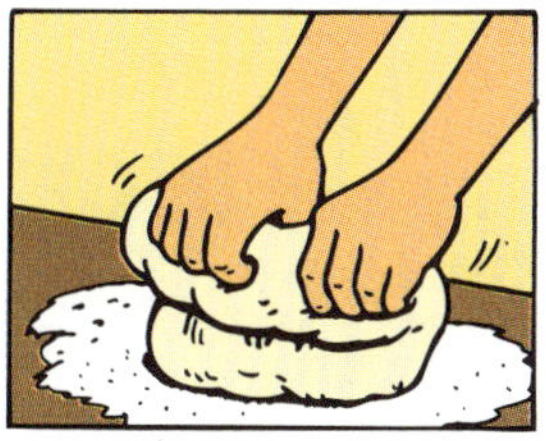

b.
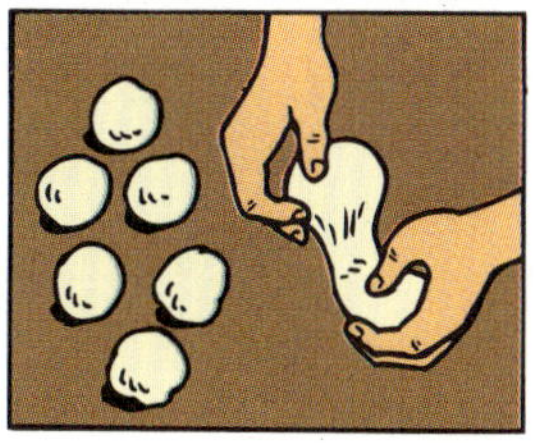

c.

d.

e.

f.

g.

h.

i.

j.

LISTENING IN. What is Tomás's problem?

Tomás: I always read the assignments, but I can't remember what I've read!

Ms. Goldstein: You need to learn how to use your textbook. You need to learn how to preread the text material. Begin by reading the chapter title. Ask yourself, "What is this chapter about?" The chapter title and the headings in the chapter give you clues.

PREREADING.

Understanding your textbook is easier when you preread an assignment. Follow these steps.

1. Begin by reading the title of the chapter. Read the boldface headings for each section.
2. Next read the introduction to the chapter as well as the chapter summary.
3. Look at any pictures, maps, graphs, or charts. Read the captions that go with these visuals.

Try the first step. Look at the textbook page. What is the title of the chapter? Read the section headings. What do you think the chapter is about?

EXPLORATION AND EXPANSION (1450-1750) 15

CHAPTER OUTLINE

1. Voyages of Exploration
2. Profitable Trade with the East
3. First Colonies in the Americas
4. Dividing up North America
5. The Commercial Revolution

The period from about 1450 to 1750 has been called the "Age of Exploration." In the 1400s, Portuguese and Spanish sailors led the way across the oceans of the world. Soon, other nations followed. Through the voyages of exploration, Europeans learned of two vast continents in the Western Hemisphere. The discovery of new ocean routes and new lands led to a race for trading empires in Asia and the Americas. This increased trade changed the economic life of Europe.

1. Voyages of Exploration

READ TO UNDERSTAND

- What new technologies helped European sailors explore the oceans of the world.
- Why Portugal and Spain led the way in exploration.

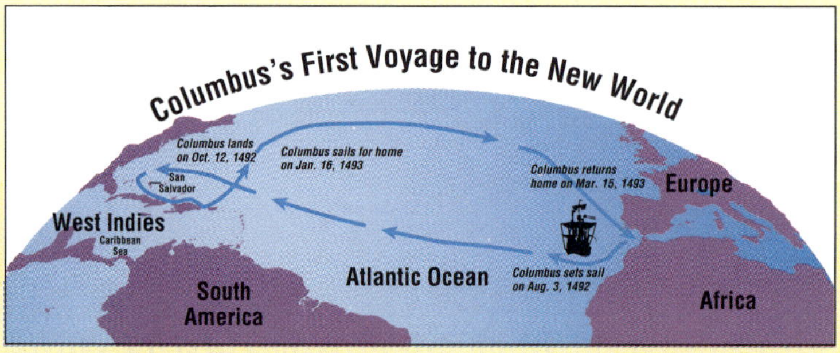

MAP STUDY: During the Age of Exploration, courageous sailors set out from Europe into the unknown.

LISTENING IN. Why are concept webs helpful?

TALKING IT OVER. Work with a partner. Talk about the topic — immigration to the United States. What concepts would you add to the concept web?

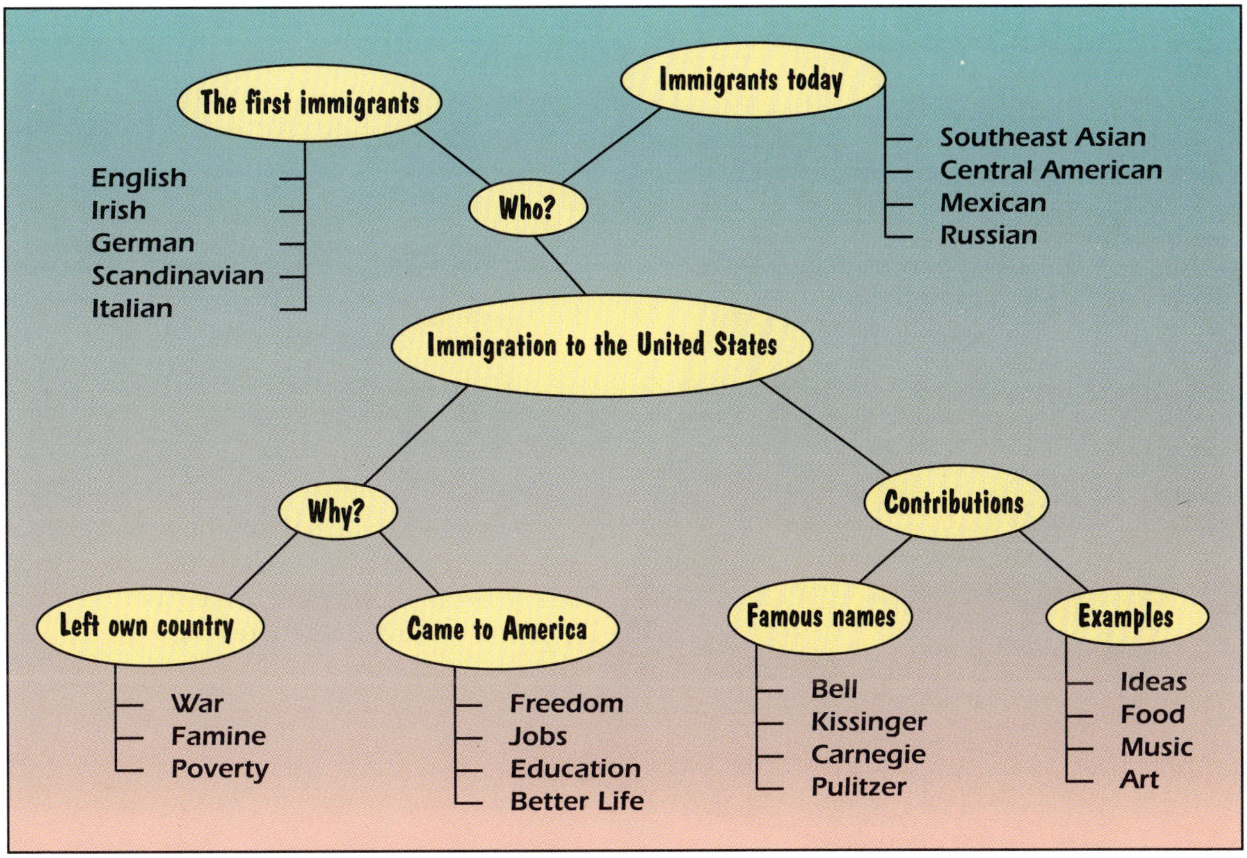

LISTENING IN.

How can tables and graphs help you?

Ms. Goldstein: Now you're ready to read. It's OK to read slowly.

Tomás: To make sure that I really understand what I'm reading, right?

Ms. Goldstein: Right! Also, be sure to look at any tables and graphs. They give you clues that help you understand.

Tomás: Tables and graphs help me "see" information in a different way.

Ms. Goldstein: Exactly! Also, ask yourself, "What am I learning? Do I understand what I'm reading?" Reread anything that you don't understand.

THINKING ABOUT IT. Make a chart that shows the main parts of a textbook and how each part helps you learn. Share your chart with your classmates.

Parts of my textbook	What each part tells me

JUST FOR Fun

Make a book cover for the textbook that you use in your favorite class. Your cover should show the reader the contents of the textbook in a creative and interesting way.

READING ABOUT IT. Read the text and the three visuals: a table, a column graph, and a pie graph.

In 1965 a new immigration law was passed by the U.S. Congress. The new law did away with quotas, which had favored immigrants from Europe.* Since 1965, our nation has experienced the largest wave of immigration since the turn of the century.

Most of the new Americans today are from Asia or a country in Latin America. Immigration from Europe has been declining.

TALKING IT OVER.

Work in a small group. Explain how the text and the visuals work together to give information. Use your own words.

TUNING IN.

Look at the information in the table. Listen to the statements. Point your thumb up if a statement is true. Point your thumb down if it is false.

THINKING ABOUT IT.

Which visual is easiest for you to understand? Explain why.

FIGURING IT OUT.

Work with a partner. Use the information in the table and the column graph to make a pie graph entitled "Immigration during the 1970s."

Immigration to the U.S.

	From Europe	From the Americas	From Asia	From Africa
1960s	1,710,000	1,120,000	420,000	30,000
1970s	800,000	1,930,000	1,630,000	90,000
1980s	640,000	2,450,000	2,695,000	170,000

TABLE

COLUMN GRAPH

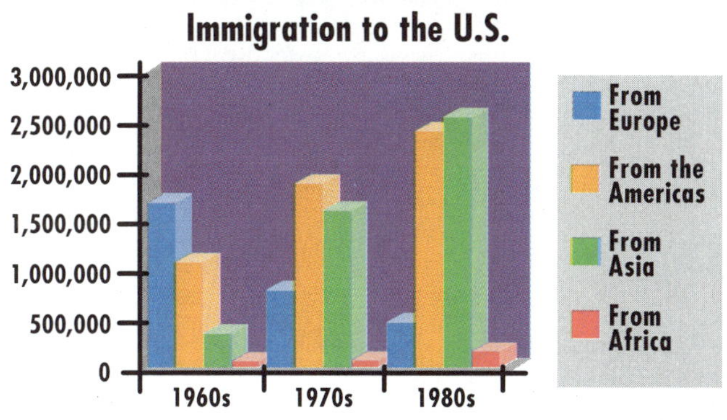

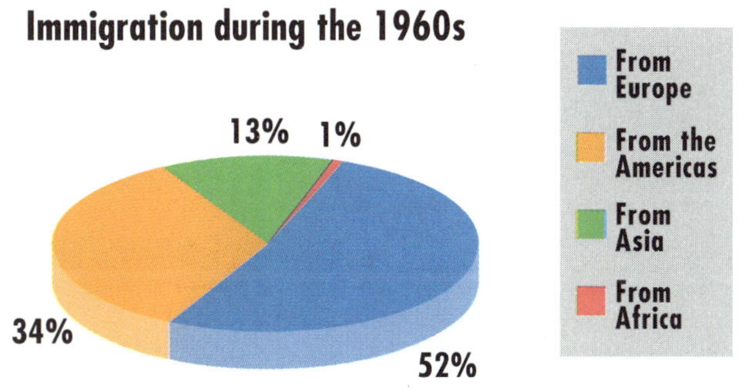

PIE GRAPH

*Note that the immigration policy of 1965 has changed.

TAKING GOOD NOTES

I. Before the lesson
- A. Get materials ready: notebook, paper, pen/pencil
- B. Put date and heading on paper
- C. Ask yourself:
  1. What is this lesson about?
  2. What do I already know?
  3. What do I need to learn?

II. During the lesson
- A. What to write down
  1. Important ideas and details
  2. Words and phrases (not sentences)
- B. Leave wide margins
  1. For your own questions
  2. For other notes
- C. Ask yourself:
  1. Do I understand this?
  2. What is important to remember?

III. After the lesson
- A. Ask yourself:
  1. Can I read my notes?
  2. Do I understand my notes?
  3. What are the important ideas?
- B. Rewrite notes if you need to
  1. Make an outline
  2. Make a mind map or concept web

Main heading
Subheading
Detail

THINKING ABOUT IT.

Find the important ideas in Ms. Goldstein's outline.

1. Underline the main headings in the outline.
2. Double underline the subheadings.
3. Circle three details.
4. Put a star next to something you already do.
5. Put a check mark next to something you should do — but usually don't do.

WRITING AND SHARING. Work with a partner. List reasons why it is important to learn to take good notes. Share your ideas with your classmates.

FIGURING IT OUT. Work in groups of three. Choose a page in a textbook. Read the information. Make either an outline or a web to organize the information. Compare your outline or web with other groups.

THINKING ABOUT IT. When might you use an outline? When might you use a web? Make a chart. Share your ideas with your classmates.

Advantages of an outline	*Advantages of a web*

LISTENING IN.

Tomás: Do you want to go to the mall?
Juan: I can't. I haven't done my math homework.
Tomás: Math? Do we have any homework in math?
Juan: Yes. And we have homework in science!
Tomás: I've already done my science homework!
Juan: I haven't. By the way, is there any homework in world history?
Tomás: Let me check my homework schedule. I make one every week.

TALKING IT OVER. Make a homework schedule for yourself for the week. Share it with a partner. Ask about his or her schedule.

TIME	Mon.	Tues.	Wed.	Thurs.	Fri.
4:00 - 5:00			history pp.75-77		
5:00 - 6:00					
6:00 - 7:00	math 1-25	ESL Portfolio		science p.53	
7:00 - 8:00	science p.52	math p.65 all	ESL Portfolio	history pp.78-80	
8:00 - 9:00	read novel	read novel	read novel	read novel	

READING ABOUT IT. Read about Neelam's study habits.

Neelam makes a homework schedule each week. She puts important assignments and tests on the schedule every day.

She begins each homework assignment by reading the directions. She asks herself, "Do I understand the assignment?"

She concentrates on her assignment. She never watches TV or listens to the radio while she is doing her homework!

When she is finished, she reads over her work again. She asks herself, "Is my homework neat? Can the teacher read it? Is it complete?"

ON YOUR OWN. Write about yourself. Describe your study habits. Then compare them to Neelam's study habits.

LISTENING IN.

Does Tomás have a good excuse for not doing his homework?

Ms. Goldstein: You didn't do your homework, Tomás? Why not?
Tomás: I have a really good excuse. Samson ate it!
Ms. Goldstein: And just who is Samson?
Tomás: My dog.
Ms. Goldstein: I need to add that to my list!

TUNING IN.

In her journal Ms. Goldstein records her students' excuses for not having their homework. Listen as she reads the list. Point your thumb up if you think the excuse is a good one. Point your thumb down if you think the excuse is a poor one.

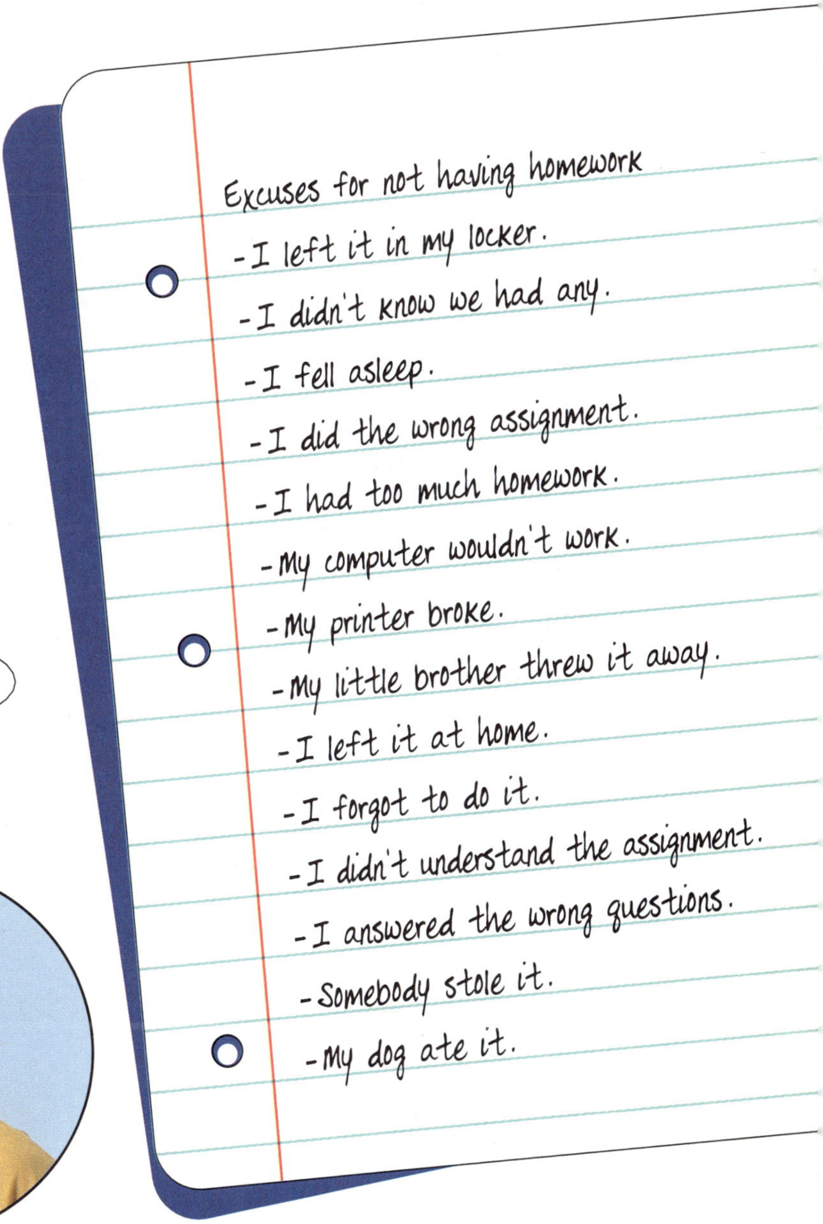

TALKING IT OVER.

Make a list of reasons why it is sometimes difficult to do your homework. Share your list with classmates and ask them for suggestions.

MS. GOLDSTEIN'S EDITING SYMBOLS

Symbol	What the symbol means	Example
sp (circled)	spelling error	Many imigrants live in California.
≡	capitalization error	Many immigrants live in california.
P	punctuation error	Many immigrants live, in California.
^	missing word	Many immigrants live California.
[ ]	extra word	Many immigrants they live in California.
V (underlined)	verb-tense error	Many immigrants are living in California.
$\overline{N}$	number singular/plural error	Many immigrants lives in California.
ww	wrong word	Much immigrants live in California.
( )?	meaning not clear	Many immigrants live in California (for the future.)?

WRITING.

Choose a piece of writing from your Portfolio. Ask your teacher to edit your writing. Then write a second draft based on your teacher's feedback.

TALKING IT OVER.

How are you doing in your classes? Talk in a small group.

UNIT 8

LET'S HAVE A PARTY FOR JUAN!

Lori: It's Juan's birthday next week. Let's have a party!
Chip: That's a great idea! Where should we have it?
Lori: We can have it at my house. I'm sure it'll be OK with my parents.
Chip: Great! Who should we invite?
Lori: Well, let's see. Michelle and Zaida and Leslie. John and David and Tran . . .
Chip: How about Neelam and Tomás?
Lori: Definitely. They're really nice.
Chip: And how about that new girl. What's her name?
Lori: Nancy Bragwell? Well . . . OK.

TUNING IN.

Listen to Lori's conversation with her mother. Then summarize what they are talking about. Use your own words.

LISTENING IN.

Is Michelle going to Juan's party?

Lori: Can you come to Juan's birthday party?
Michelle: I don't know. I haven't asked my stepfather yet.
Lori: Why not?
Michelle: I'm afraid he'll say no.
Lori: Why?
Michelle: He doesn't like the idea of boy-girl parties. He says I'm too young.

ACTING IT OUT.

You have been invited to Juan's party. You really want to go, but first you need to ask permission.

▲ What will you say?

▲ How many ways do you know to ask permission?

▲ What do you think is the best way to ask?

Practice asking for permission with a partner.

WRITING AND SHARING.

You want to go to a boy-girl party. What questions do you think an adult in your family might ask? What answers would you have ready? Make a list. Then share your list with your classmates.

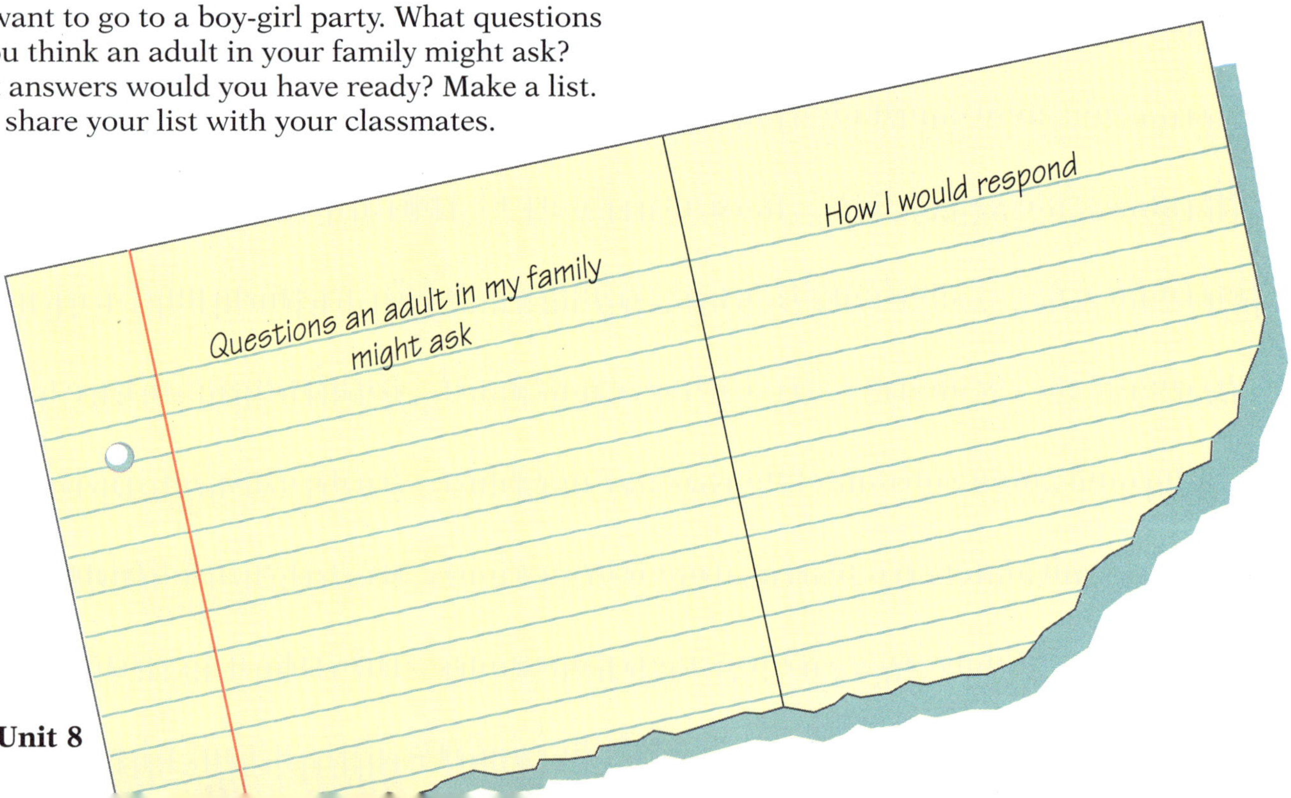

LISTENING IN.

What are the students trying to do?

Michelle: My stepfather's going to let me go!
Lori: Great! You can help us plan the party.
Michelle: What kind of food should we have?
Chip: Well, how about a birthday . . .
Michelle: Quiche! Let's have . . . !
Lori: What a dumb idea! That's adult food!
Michelle: Well, how about . . .
Chip: What kinds of music should we . . . ?
Michelle: Mutant Teenage . . .
Lori: Did you hear what happened to their drummer?
Chip: I think I'll wear my new . . .
Lori: What's wrong with us? We're all talking at once. We'll never plan the party this way!

READING ABOUT IT. It can be difficult to work as a group. Groups usually work better when their members follow a set of rules. When you work in a group, remember to follow these eight important rules.

1. Don't interrupt others.
2. Take turns.
3. Avoid "put-downs."
4. Keep to the subject.
5. Don't argue.
6. Let others take credit.
7. Accept other people's ideas.
8. Listen to other people.

TUNING IN.

Listen to Lori, Chip, and Michelle's conversation. Which rules are they breaking?

TALKING IT OVER.

How well do you work in a group? Work with three or four classmates to plan a surprise party. Discuss the questions on the list. Remember the rules for working in a group!

- *Who will we invite?*
- *When will we have the party?*
- *Where will we have the party?*
- *Will we serve food? What kind?*
- *Will we have decorations? What kind?*
- *Will we have entertainment? What kind?*
- *What special activities will we have?*

LISTENING IN.

Has Lori picked up the birthday cake?

Michelle: Are you ready for the party?
Lori: Let me check the list.
Michelle: Have you picked up the cake yet?
Lori: No. I'll pick it up this afternoon.
Michelle: Have you put up the decorations?
Lori: Not yet. I'll put them up in a few minutes.
Michelle: Have you made the refreshments?
Lori: Everything's in the fridge. I still have to make the dips, though.
Michelle: Well, let me know if I can help with anything!

THINGS TO DO!!!!!

- *Order cake*
- *Buy decorations*
- *Clean the house*
- *Put up decorations*
- *Pick up cake*
- *Buy food*
- *Buy drinks*
- *Make ice*
- *Get tapes and CDs from Chip*
- *Get clothes ready*

TALKING IT OVER.

It's almost three o'clock, and the party starts at seven o'clock. Read the conversation again. Look at Lori's list. Is Lori ready for the party? What has she already done? What does she still have to do?

THINKING ABOUT IT.

Make a list of things Lori forgot to put on her list. Then share your list with a partner.

TUNING IN. Listen to Juan and his uncle's conversation. If you agree with a suggestion that Uncle Carlos makes, point your thumb up. If you disagree, point your thumb down.

TALKING IT OVER. Juan has many questions about the party. Work in a small group. Give advice. Make suggestions.

THINKING ABOUT IT. Compare party etiquette in the United States to etiquette in your culture. How are the "rules" the same? How are they different? Talk with your classmates.

LISTENING IN. What is a navigator? Find out.

Juan: I'm sorry I'm late!
Lori: We were getting worried. Did you have trouble following my directions?
Juan: No. It was my fault. I was the navigator.
Lori: Well, anyway, you're here. Hey, everybody, the birthday boy is here!

TUNING IN.

Look at the map. Listen as Juan gives directions to his uncle. Follow along on the map. Which directions are wrong?

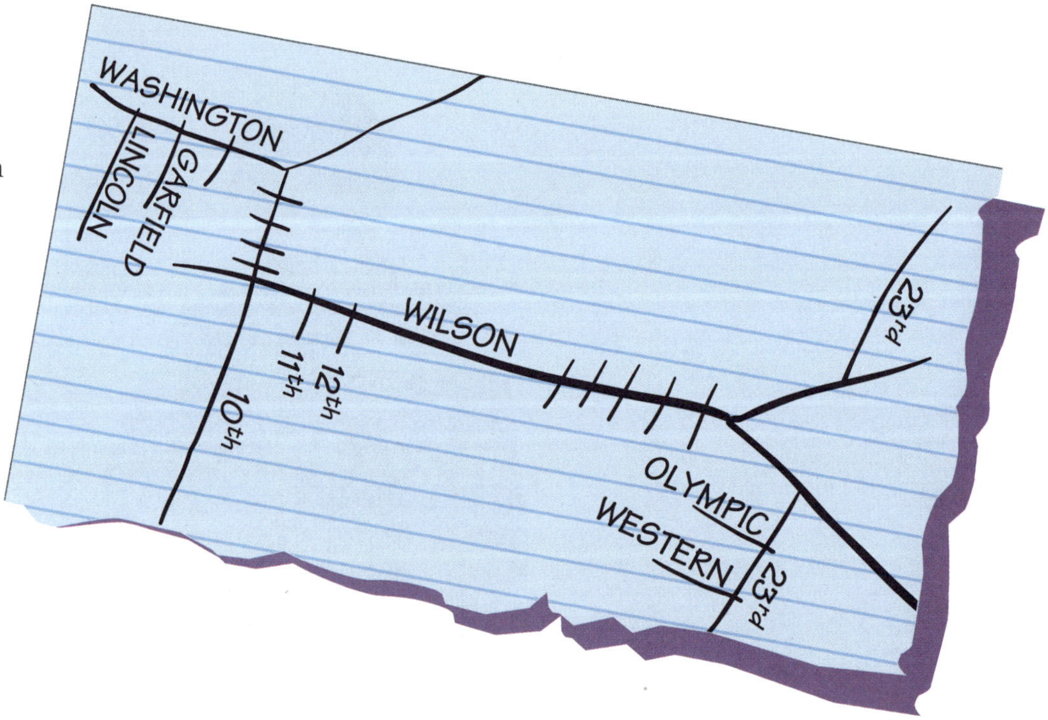

JUST FOR Fun

Work with a partner. Ask each other where you live. Then draw maps that show how to get from your partner's house or apartment to yours.

LISTENING IN.

Is Nancy Bragwell a new student at Kennedy?

Chip: This is Nancy Bragwell. She just transferred to Kennedy from Fairlawn Junior High.
Juan: Hi, Nancy. Nice to meet you . . . Lori's apartment is really nice, isn't it?
Nancy: I guess, but it's a bit small.
Juan: Is your place larger?
Nancy: Much larger. We have four bedrooms and two baths. We have one of the largest apartments in the neighborhood.
Juan: Oh, well . . .

TALKING IT OVER.

Here are the floor plans for the Chans' apartment and for the Bragwells' apartment. Compare the two apartments. Which do you prefer? Why?

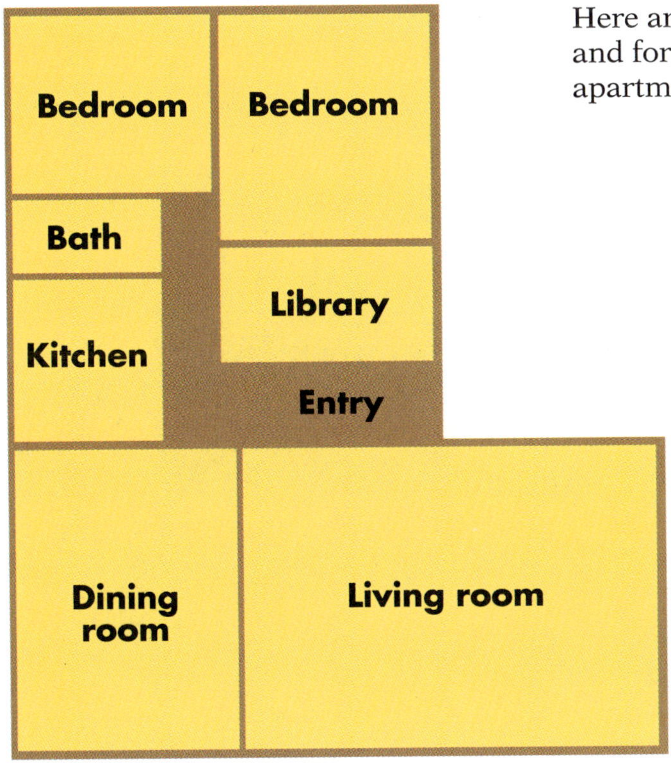

The Chan Family's Apartment

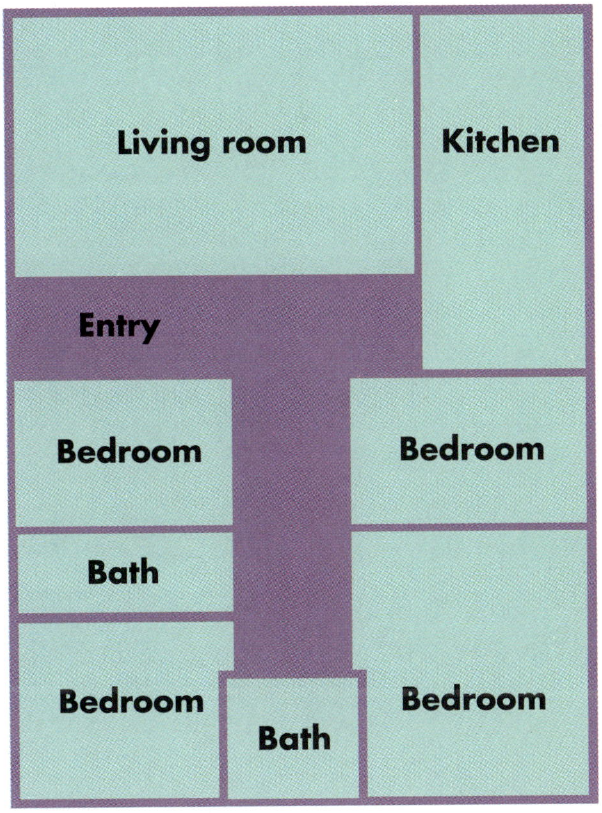

The Bragwell Family's Apartment

TUNING IN.

Listen as Lori describes her apartment. Follow along on the floor plan.

LISTENING IN. Why do you think Michelle wants to talk to Juan and Chip?

Michelle: This is a great party!
Nancy: It's OK, I guess.
Michelle: The food is fantastic.
Nancy: Have you tried the guacamole? It's way too salty.
Michelle: Oh, well, this music is fabulous! Do you like the Noise Boys?
Nancy: This isn't the Noise Boys! It's Men Out of Work.
Michelle: It is? I thought . . .
Nancy: They don't even sound the same!
Michelle: Yeah, I guess they don't. By the way, I'm looking for a CD player. Have you looked for one recently? Do you have any recommendations?
Nancy: How much do you want to spend?
Michelle: About fifty dollars.
Nancy: Ha! You're not going to find anything good at that price!
Michelle: Uh . . . Have you seen Juan and Chip? I'd like to talk to them.
Nancy: Juan and Chip. What for?
Michelle: What do you mean, what for?
Nancy: Those two are such . . . well . . . you know!

ACTING IT OUT. Work with a partner. Rewrite the conversation between Nancy and Michelle so that Nancy says things that would make other people enjoy being with her and talking to her. Then act out the new conversation for your classmates.

TUNING IN. Listen to Zaida and Nancy's conversation. Then act it out with a partner.

LISTENING IN. Who are Michelle and Chip talking about?

Michelle: What's wrong with Nancy? I just can't stand her!
Chip: Nobody can.
Michelle: Have you noticed how negative she is about everything?
Chip: And a know-it-all, too!
Michelle: I don't like her constant put-downs.
Chip: Me neither.
Michelle: By the way, did you hear why she transferred out of Fairlawn?
Chip: She said that Kennedy is closer to her home.
Michelle: Well, I heard that the principal caught her . . . I better whisper it . . .
Chip: That's just a rumor! I don't think it's true.

TALKING IT OVER. Talk with a partner.

- ▲ Why does Michelle think that Nancy is negative?
- ▲ Why does Chip say that she is a know-it-all?
- ▲ What are some examples of Nancy's put-downs?

THINKING ABOUT IT.

Gossip is the spreading of rumors — usually about other people. Gossip can be very harmful. Why do you think this is true? Make a list of reasons why people shouldn't gossip. Share your list with your classmates.

ON YOUR OWN.

Do you sometimes hear put-downs in conversations at your school? List some examples of put-downs. Share and discuss them with your classmates.

LISTENING IN.

In the game Charades, what do the teams write on slips of paper?

Lori: Does anybody want to play Charades? It's a really fun game!
Juan: What's Charades and how do you play it?
Lori: I'll explain it to you. There are two teams. Each team thinks of titles of books or movies and writes each title on a slip of paper. Someone — for example, Michelle — picks a slip of paper from the other team. Then she acts out the title, and the other members of her team try to guess what it is.
Chip: And she can't talk!
Lori: And her team has to guess in 60 seconds or less!
Michelle: The team with the most correct guesses wins.

JUST FOR Fun

Work in a small group. Create a party game. Think about these questions.

▲ How many people can play?
▲ What are the rules?
▲ Is time important?
▲ How do you win?

Make a chart that shows how to play the game. Then explain the game to your classmates.

THINKING ABOUT IT. Here is a list of books that are popular with preteens and teens. Which book titles do you think would be good choices for Charades? Why?

- Are You There God? It's Me, Margaret
- The Cat Ate My Gymsuit
- Island of the Blue Dolphins
- My Darling, My Hamburger
- Otherwise Known as Sheila the Great
- The Outsiders
- Pardon Me, You're Stepping on My Eyeball
- The Red Pony
- Seven Days to a Brand-New Me
- Sherlock Holmes Through Time and Space
- The Summer of the Swans
- Tales of a Fourth Grade Nothing
- Treasure Island
- The Trouble with Thirteen

TALKING IT OVER.

Work with two or three classmates who like the same kinds of books or movies as you do — mysteries, adventure stories, and so forth. Write five titles on slips of paper that would make good choices for a game of Charades.

ACTING IT OUT.

Play a class game of Charades! Use titles of books or movies.

ON YOUR OWN.

Design a funny birthday card. Share it with your classmates.

TALKING IT OVER.

Help Juan decide what to do now. Give advice. Make suggestions.

FINDING OUT. Find out how to say "Happy Birthday" in another language. Teach your classmates.

UNIT 9

WHAT ARE FAMILIES FOR, ANYWAY?

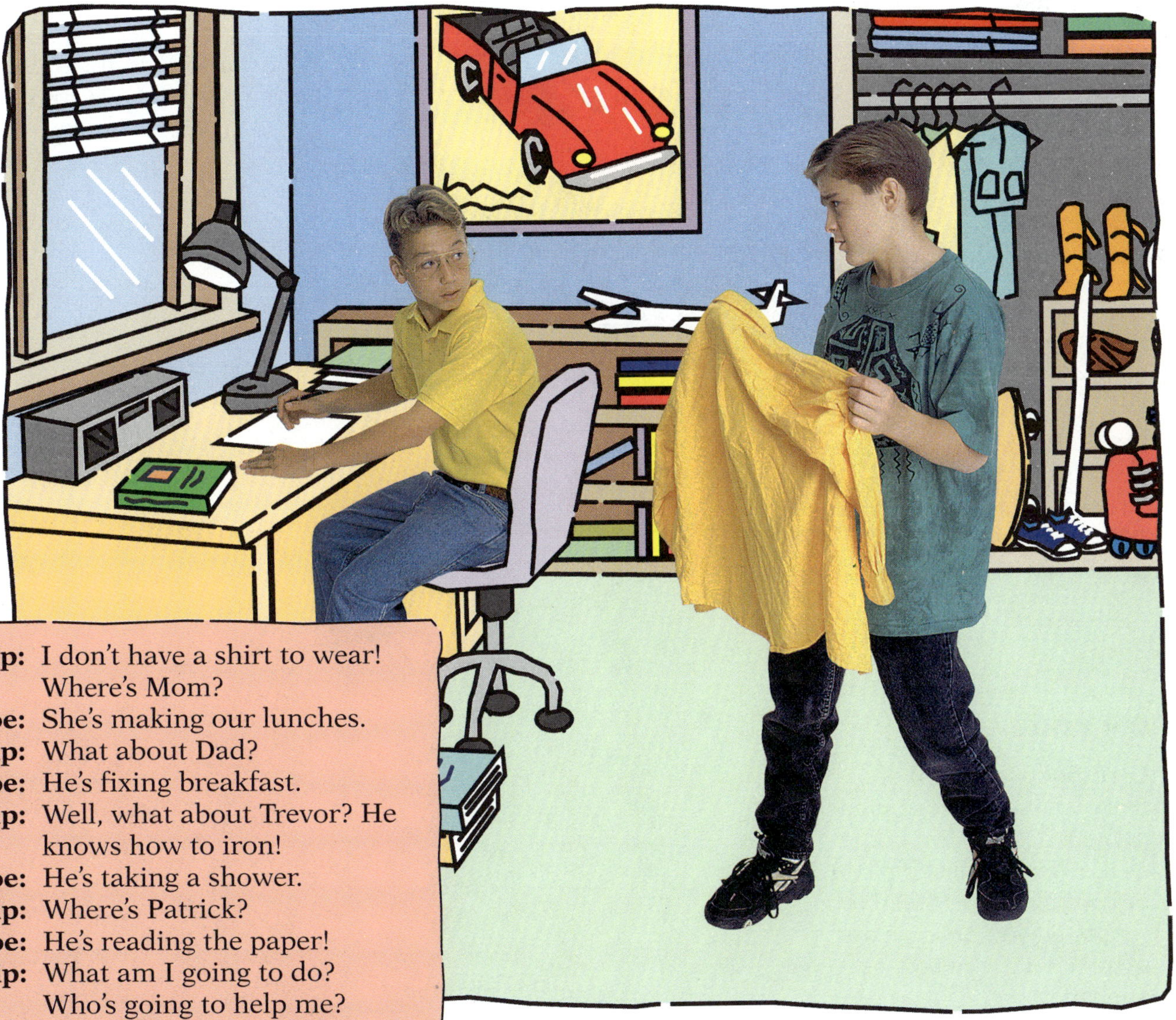

Chip: I don't have a shirt to wear! Where's Mom?
Joe: She's making our lunches.
Chip: What about Dad?
Joe: He's fixing breakfast.
Chip: Well, what about Trevor? He knows how to iron!
Joe: He's taking a shower.
Chip: Where's Patrick?
Joe: He's reading the paper!
Chip: What am I going to do? Who's going to help me?
Joe: Not me! I'm finishing my book report. It's due tomorrow.
Chip: What are families for, anyway?
Joe: I guess you'd better learn how to use an iron!

TUNING IN. Listen to the rest of the conversation. Then summarize it in your own words.

LISTENING IN. What does Mr. Kowalski say Chip is good at?

THINKING ABOUT IT.

Think about Chip's question "What are families for, anyway?" Make a list of things that members of your family do for each other. Then share your list with your classmates.

ON YOUR OWN.

Careful observation of a place, person, or event can make a description come to life. Write a description of your classroom. Use your senses as you observe and record what you see, hear and smell.

When you're finished writing your description, compare observations with a partner. Did you include details that your partner did not?

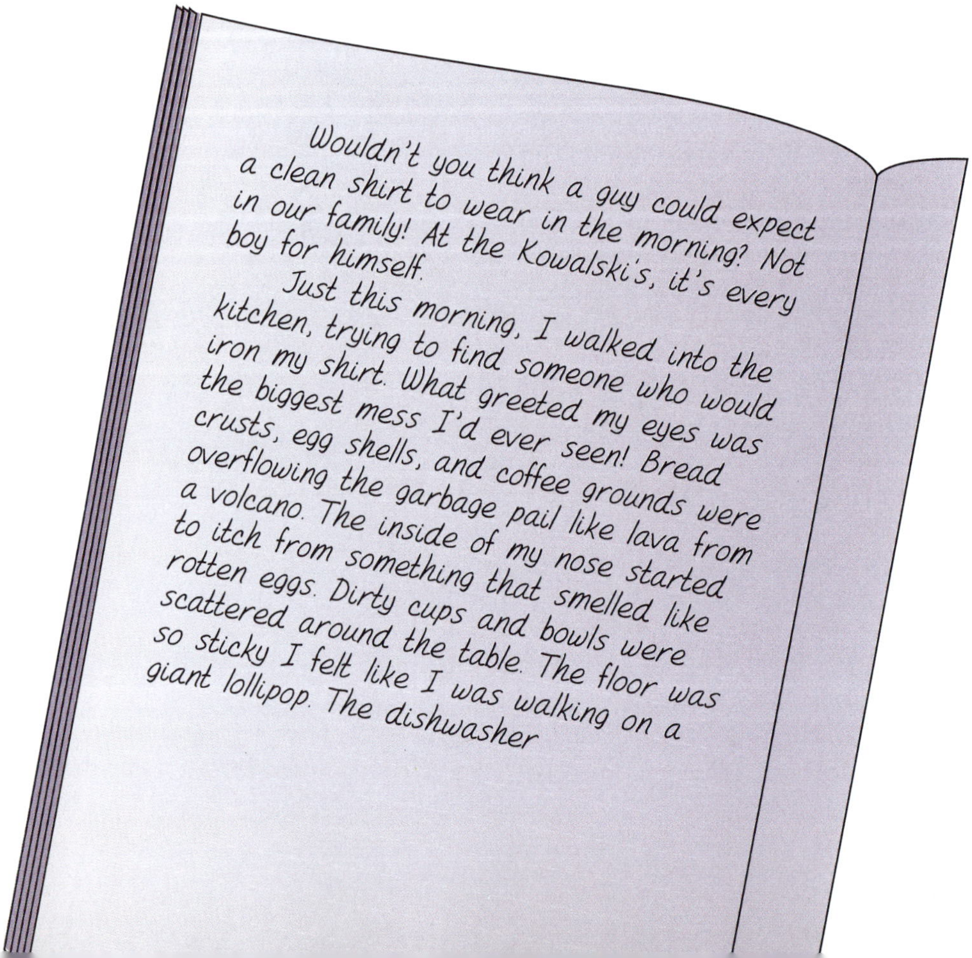

TUNING IN. Look at the picture. What jobs need to be done? Listen to Mr. Kowalski and point to the part of the picture that matches his words.

ACTING IT OUT. Pretend that you are either Mr. Kowalski or Mrs. Kowalski. Tell your sons what jobs need to be done. Ask politely for their help.

LISTENING IN.

Which chore can be done very quickly?

THINKING ABOUT IT.

Are there chores you enjoy doing? Are there chores you don't mind doing? Are there chores you really dislike doing? Make a chart.

Chores I like	Chores I don't mind	Chores I don't like

FINDING OUT.

Take a survey to find out which household chores you and your classmates like least. Begin by making a list of common chores. Make a column graph to show the results.

1. making breakfast
2. helping to make dinner
3. doing the dishes
4. taking out the garbage
5. dusting
6. vacuuming
7. doing the laundry
8. unloading the dishwasher
9. folding and sorting clothes
10. ironing clothes
11. mowing the lawn
12. running errands
13. cleaning the garage
14. walking the dog

ACTING IT OUT. Pretend that you are one of the Kowalski brothers. Make a deal. Offer to help out in exchange for a favor.

THINKING ABOUT IT. Some families pay their children for the household chores they perform. Work with a partner. Make a chart that shows what you think various household chores are worth.

Chore	Dollar value	Reason

ON YOUR OWN. Invent a new household tool or appliance that would "revolutionize" your chores. Be creative. Draw and label your invention. Be ready to tell your classmates what your invention is for, how it works, and why it's special.

LISTENING IN.

What does Joe say about doing the dishes?

Joe: Doing the dishes is a girl's job. I don't want to do it.
Mrs. Kowalski: What was that?
Joe: I said doing the dishes is a girl's job.
Mrs. Kowalski: We don't have girl's jobs and boy's jobs in this family.
Joe: Oh, all right. But when is someone going to fix the dishwasher?
Chip: When is someone going to iron my shirt?

TALKING IT OVER. Work with a partner or in a small group. Compare the unwritten rules about boys and girls in the majority U.S. culture to your culture. Make a chart.

	It's OK for girls to ...	It's OK for boys to ...
In the majority U.S. culture		
In the ______ culture		

ACTING IT OUT. Work with a partner. Rewrite the conversation between Joe and Mrs. Kowalski. If you'd like, you can change the characters. Then act out the new conversation.

TUNING IN. Look at the pictures. Listen to the statements about boys and girls. If you agree with a statement, point your thumb up. If you disagree with it, point your thumb down.

TALKING IT OVER. Discuss these questions with your classmates.

- ▲ Do you avoid taking some courses at school just because you are a boy or a girl? If so, what courses?
- ▲ Are there activities at school that are mostly for girls or mostly for boys? Do you think it is a good idea to have these kinds of activities? Why or why not?

LISTENING IN.

What do Mr. and Mrs. Kowalski share?

Mr. Kowalski: Your mother and I share the responsibility of raising you boys.
Patrick: I know, but I still don't believe that men should do housework.
Mr. Kowalski: You don't think I should clean the house when it's a mess?
Patrick: Well . . . I guess that's OK.
Mr. Kowalski: Or cook your dinner when you're hungry?
Patrick: Hmmm . . . that's definitely OK!

	Percentage who say they do all or most household jobs	Percentage who say they share household jobs equally with partner
Cleaning house or apartment		
Women	89	9
Men	5	15
Cooking meals		
Women	90	7
Men	5	10
Disciplining children		
Women	35	61
Men	14	72
Doing laundry		
Women	93	5
Men	5	7
Grocery Shopping		
Women	82	13
Men	8	21
Fixing things around the house		
Women	9	17
Men	86	10

THINKING ABOUT IT.

Many people believe that both partners should share the responsibility for doing household chores. A recent study shows, however, that most families in the United States are very traditional when it comes to who does what around the house.

What do the data in the table show? In your own words, explain the study's findings.

FIGURING IT OUT. Make a graph that presents the information in the table.

ON YOUR OWN. Design a survey about family roles and responsibilities. Give your survey to at least ten people. Then use a table or graph to report your results.

TUNING IN.

Listen to the statements about men's and women's roles and responsibilities. If you agree with a statement, point your thumb up. If you disagree with it, point your thumb down.

Chores and Activities

- mow the lawn
- arrange flowers
- clean the garage
- wash dishes
- prepare meals
- read romance novels
- watch football on TV
- sew or knit
- repair things
- clean the bathroom
- pay bills
- go grocery shopping
- do the laundry
- shovel snow
- wash windows
- collect stamps
- wax the floor
- make the bed
- dust the furniture
- hunt and fish

FINDING OUT.

Ask the adults in your family which roles and responsibilities they think are men's and which they think are women's. Arrange their answers in a chart. Do you agree with the adults in your family? Explain and discuss your chart with your classmates.

Roles for men only	Roles for women only

LISTENING IN.

Does Chip like to fix things?

Chip:	I'll help you fix the dishwasher, Mom. Fixing things isn't work. It's play.
Mrs. Kowalski:	Glad to hear that. After you're done, you can take out the trash.
Chip:	Forget it! Taking out the trash is work!
Mrs. Kowalski:	So is fixing your dinner, sweetheart.
Chip:	By the way, do I have an ironed shirt to wear tomorrow?

TALKING IT OVER.

Describe the common household jobs that you do. Use the words from the list.

boring	filthy
challenging	fun
dangerous	hard
demanding	interesting
difficult	menial
dirty	routine
easy	tedious
enjoyable	tiring

THINKING ABOUT IT.

Make a list of typical household activities. Tell if you think each one is "work" or "play." Then share your list with your classmates.

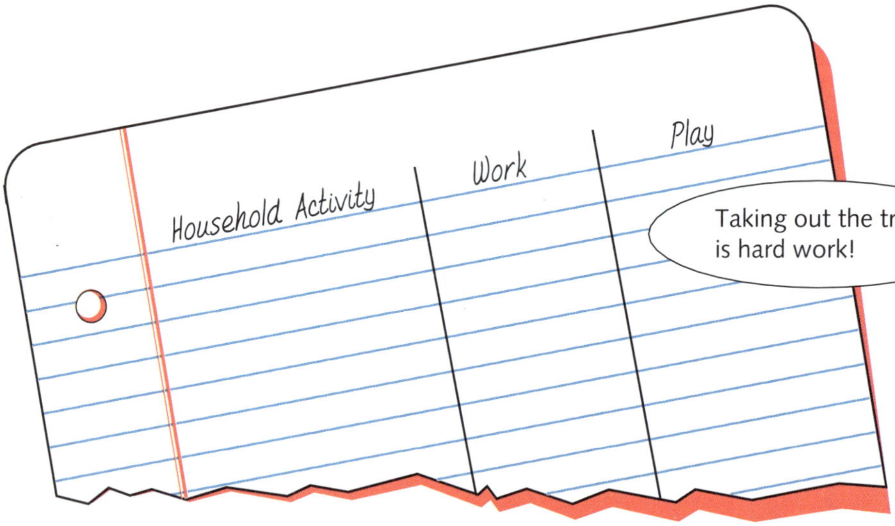

JUST FOR Fun

Draw two pictures of your family. In the first picture, show your family at work. In the second, show your family having fun. Share your drawings with your classmates.

LISTENING IN.

What does Chip say he is too young to do?

Mrs. Kowalski: It's interesting, Chip, that you can fix a dishwasher, but you can't iron a shirt.
Chip: I don't know how to iron.
Mrs. Kowalski: I'll show you how.
Chip: But I'm too young to do ironing!
Mrs. Kowalski: You're too young to iron . . . but you're old enough to fix a dishwasher?
Chip: OK. If you show me how to iron, I'll show you how to fix a dishwasher.

GIVING DIRECTIONS.

Work with a partner. First review the steps for giving good directions on page 75. Then take turns playing the role of Chip. Tell him how to do the following.

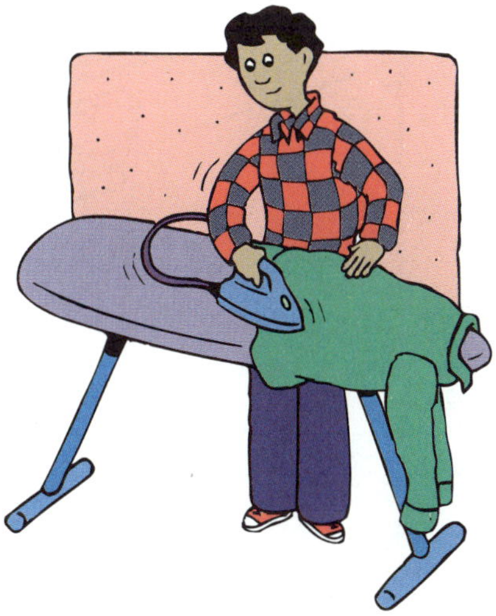

- ▲ iron a shirt
- ▲ sort the laundry
- ▲ make the bed
- ▲ make a sandwich
- ▲ load the dishwasher
- ▲ wash the car

THINKING ABOUT IT. Do you think Chip is too young to learn to iron? Make a chart that shows what chores kids at different ages can do.

Chores a five-year-old can do	Chores an eight-year-old can do	Chores kids my age can do	Chores that I'm still too young to do

LISTENING IN. Do you think Chip wants to put away the tools?

Mrs. Kowalski: Thanks for fixing the dishwasher. I'm really proud of you!
Chip: And thanks for teaching me how to iron, Mom. You're the best!
Mrs. Kowalski: You know, I really appreciate your help.
Chip: I know. Now can I go over to Juan's?
Mrs. Kowalski: Sure, right after you put away the tools you've left lying all over the floor.
Chip: Why can't someone else put away the tools?

TUNING IN. Listen to the rest of the conversation. Do you agree with Chip? Why or why not?

FIGURING IT OUT. The tools are spread out on the kitchen floor. Do you know what they are? Which tools do you think Chip actually used to fix the dishwasher?

UNIT 10

WHAT'S HAPPENING TO MY BODY?

TUNING IN. Listen in on the students' private thoughts. For each thought, write a plus sign (+) if it's a concern for you, too. Write a minus sign (–) if it's not a concern.

READING ABOUT IT.

Read about the changes that girls and boys experience during adolescence.

Many girls your age develop acne. The oil glands in the skin begin to produce more oil and often become clogged. Your skin "breaks out." Wash with a mild soap and use water-based make-up.

Girls your age start to notice body odor. Bathe or shower daily and use a deodorant.

Girls start to grow taller at age eleven or twelve. They stop growing taller at about age sixteen.

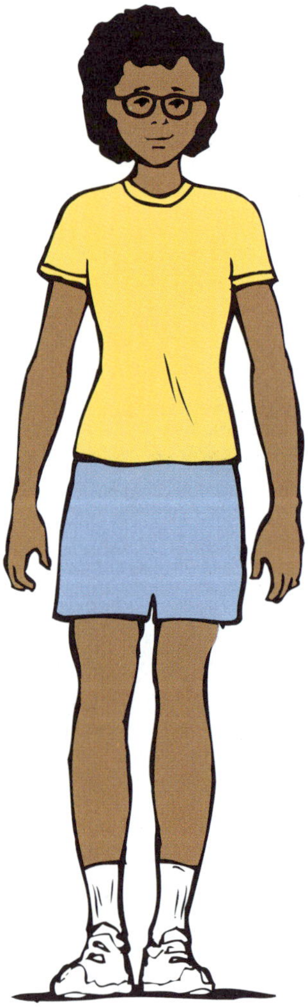

Most girls' breasts start to grow at age eleven or twelve. Each girl develops at her own rate. Breast size is a family trait.

Most girls' bodies are prepared to have babies by the age of twelve. It is important for you to understand the "facts of life."

Most girls also get body hair around age eleven or twelve. Body hair is a family trait, too.

Girls start to gain weight — especially in the hips, thighs, and upper arms.

TALKING IT OVER. Work with a partner. Kids your age often are embarrassed to take showers in PE. Make a list of the pros and cons of making kids shower in PE. If you could make the policy for your school, what would you decide? Why?

TUNING IN. Listen to the conversation between Juan and his uncle. What should Juan do? Give him advice.

Boys often develop acne, just like girls. Acne usually clears up by the late teens. Consult a doctor if the acne is severe.

One in four teenagers needs glasses. Eyes should be checked regularly.

Boys' voices change at about age twelve. Their voices get deeper as they grow older.

Most boys gain from 30 to 50 pounds between the ages of twelve and eighteen.

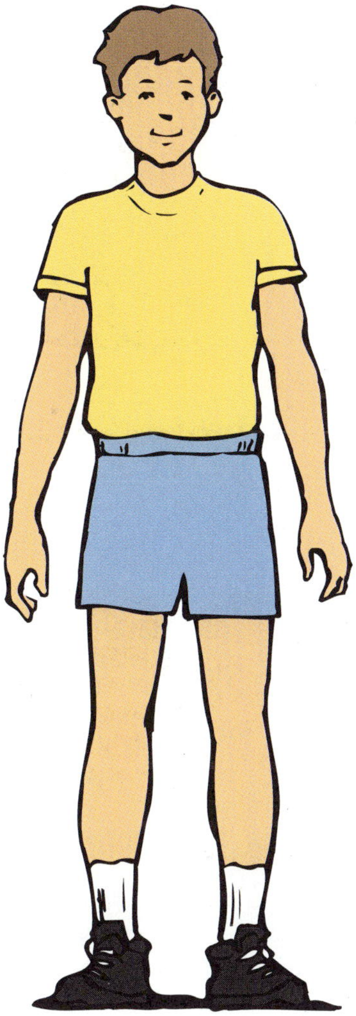

Boys' muscle bulk — the size of their muscles — becomes greater at age fourteen or fifteen. Their shoulders become broader. Their legs and arms get bigger.

Most boys are able to father children by the time they are fourteen. Both boys and girls need to understand the risks of being sexually active.

Most boys grow taller a little later than girls do. Males often keep growing into their twenties.

Boys usually develop body hair a little later than girls.

THINKING ABOUT IT. Many grooming products advertised in popular magazines are aimed at teenage readers. Find an advertisement that targets a concern kids have about their growing bodies. Show it to your classmates and talk about it. Does the ad make you want to buy the product? Why or why not?

LISTENING IN. Why does Mr. Fields say "very funny" to Chip?

Mr. Fields: Growing bodies need good food. You need to eat right.
Michelle: How do we make sure that our diet is healthy?
Mr. Fields: Good question. Have you ever heard of the four basic food groups? You're nodding your head, Chip.
Chip: Take out, delivered, canned, and frozen!
Mr. Fields: Very funny. We used to think that each food group was equally important. Let's look at the traditional food groups.

READING ABOUT IT. Read the pie chart and the examples.

Ice cream belongs to the milk and dairy products group. So does yogurt.

Noodles belong to the bread and cereal group. So does rice.

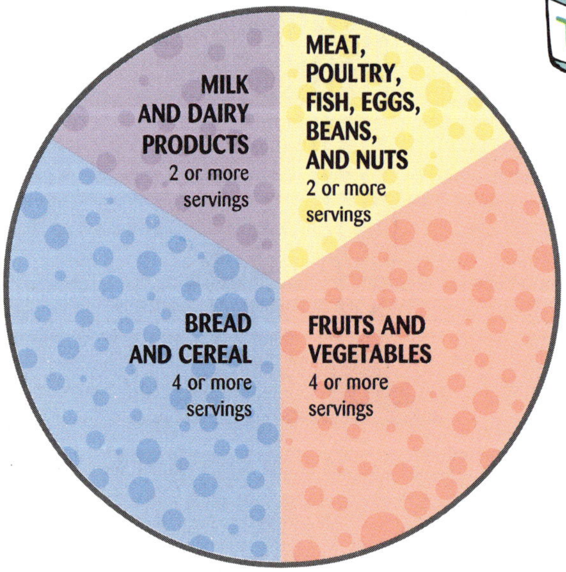

THE TRADITIONAL BASIC FOUR FOOD GROUPS

Tuna belongs to the meat and fish group. So do eggs.

Broccoli, carrots, and corn all belong to the fruit and vegetable group. So do apples.

TALKING IT OVER. List foods that you eat during a typical day. In which traditional food group or groups does each belong?

THINKING ABOUT IT.

Why do you think the Eating-Right Pyramid is a better guide for a balanced diet than the traditional four food groups?

FIGURING IT OUT.

Work with a partner. Design a one-day menu that is based on the Eating-Right Pyramid. Remember to give the serving size for each item on your menu.

half a cup of rice

a slice of whole wheat bread

a medium apple

three ounces of turkey

half a cup of corn

two slices of cheese

one cup of milk

FINDING OUT. Work with two or three classmates who come from different cultures. Make an eating-right pyramid that includes examples of dishes from these cultures.

ON YOUR OWN.

Follow Mr. Fields's directions.

	Bread, cereal, grains, and pasta	Vegetables	Fruits	Meat, poultry, fish, beans, eggs, and nuts	Milk, yogurt, and cheese	Fats, oils, and sweets
Servings needed each day	*6–11*	*3–5*	*2–4*	*2–3*	*2–3*	*Very little!*
Breakfast						
Lunch						
Dinner						
Snacks						

TALKING IT OVER. First compare charts with a classmate. Whose diet is healthier — yours or your classmate's? Why? Next tell your classmates what you eat on a typical day. Does everyone eat breakfast? Why is it important to eat a good breakfast? What are some reasons people give for not eating breakfast?

LISTENING IN.

What is one reason Kennedy has a closed campus at lunch?

Mr. Fields: Kids your age often eat too much junk food. That's one reason we have a closed campus at lunch.
Juan: Yeah! We can't go to the Fast-Food Palace!
Mr. Fields: Our school lunch helps provide you with a balanced diet.
Chip: But I like junk food!
John: Me, too! Cheddar cheese potato chips are my favorite!

FIGURING IT OUT.

Work with a partner. Analyze Kennedy's lunch menu. Explain why the menu is balanced.

TUNING IN.

Chip and John are eating lunch together. Listen to their conversation. Who has the healthier lunch? Why?

Menu

Group 1: ENTREES
Burrito
BBQ Chicken Sandwich
Chicken Pattie on a Bun
Cold Sandwich on White or Whole Wheat
Hamburger on a Bun
Cheeseburger on a Bun
Hot Dog on a Bun
Hot Pastrami & Cheese on Rye
Ham & Turkey Melt on Toast
Hot Ham & Cheese on a Croissant
Pepperoni Pizza
Tostizza (Mexican Pizza)

DAILY SPECIALS

Monday	Torpedo Submarine
Tuesday	Macaroni & Cheese w/Ham
Wednesday	Chicken Chow Mein
Thursday	Super Burrito
Friday	Taco Salad

Group 2: FRUIT
Fresh Fruit in Season
Chilled Fruit Cup
Frozen Fruit Shape-up
Fruit Juice (4 oz.)
Grape, Apple, Orange, Pineapple Orange, or Fruit Punch

Group 3: VEGETABLES
Tossed Green Salad
Hot Vegetable of the Day
French Fries

Group 4: MILK/DAIRY
Low Fat Milk
Whole Milk
Chocolate Milk

JUST FOR Fun

Visit your local supermarket. Check where various kinds of junk food are located. Why do you think the junk foods are put in certain places? Report your findings to your classmates.

Push-ups are good for both the upper arms and chest.

Pull-ups are good for the lower arms.

ON YOUR OWN.

Read about the benefits of exercise. As you read, think about your own fitness habits. How do you get your exercise?

Sit-ups are good for the stomach and lower back.

Running is good for the heart.

Riding a bike is good for the legs.

FINDING OUT.

Work with three or four classmates who all share the same favorite sport. Make a chart or poster that shows why that sport is good for the body. Be ready to share what you've learned with your classmates.

TUNING IN.

Lori and Michelle are talking about sports and activities. Listen in on their conversation. Which activity do you think Lori should choose?

SPORT ACTIVITY	Strengthens heart	Builds muscles	Helps control weight
Basketball	*Excellent*	*Poor*	*Fair*
Bicycling	*Excellent*	*Good*	*Excellent*
Bowling	*Poor*	*Poor*	*Poor*
Fast dancing	*Good*	*Poor*	*Good*
Football	*Fair*	*Good*	*Fair*
Gymnastics	*Fair*	*Excellent*	*Fair*
Running	*Excellent*	*Poor*	*Good*
Soccer	*Excellent*	*Poor*	*Good*
Softball	*Poor*	*Poor*	*Fair*
Swimming	*Excellent*	*Fair*	*Excellent*
Tennis	*Fair*	*Poor*	*Fair*
Tumbling	*Good*	*Good*	*Fair*
Volleyball	*Fair*	*Fair*	*Fair*
Walking	*Fair*	*Poor*	*Fair*

ON YOUR OWN.

A learning log is an "academic journal" that helps you think about what you already know and understand new things that you are learning.

Begin a separate log for one subject you're taking. Use spiral-bound notebooks.

- ▲ The learning log is for you. Include ideas and facts that you find interesting, important, or worth remembering.
- ▲ As you write each entry, tell where you got the information and why you think it is important.
- ▲ Log entries are informal. Include lists, charts, drawings, webs — whatever helps you remember and understand new ideas and connect one idea to another.
- ▲ Include special notes and questions to yourself — especially when you want to learn more or when you are not sure you understand the new information.

AEROBICS (noun). Exercises involving the intake of large amounts of oxygen for long periods of time. Learned in health class today that lots of "fun" activities provide the same benefits as aerobics exercises.

(FIND OUT: Why is it important to get oxygen?)

LISTENING IN.

What is Mr. Fields going to help the students design?

Mr. Fields: Some of you might want to set up a fitness program.
Chip: How much exercise do we need?
Mr. Fields: A more important question is "How often?" You need a routine. You need to exercise your body three or four times a week for at least thirty minutes.
Juan: What exercises should we do?
Mr. Fields: Find exercises and activities that you enjoy. I can help you design an exercise program.

TUNING IN.

What exercises and activities might you enjoy? Listen to Chip's suggestions. For each suggestion, point your thumb up if you think you would enjoy the activity. Point your thumb down if you don't think you would enjoy it.

TALKING IT OVER.

Talk with your classmates. Describe warm-up and stretching activities you might include in an exercise program. Describe some aerobic activities. Suggest possible ways to reward yourself for following the program.

• EXERCISE PROGRAM •

Name: ______________________

Time each day: __________ Time each week: __________

Activities

Warm-up activities:

____

____

How long: ______________________

Stretching activities: ______________________

____

How long: ______________________

Aerobic activities: ______________________

____

How long: ______________________

Reward each day: ______________________

____

Signature

FINDING OUT. Jogging is a popular aerobic activity. What are some of the important *do's* and *don'ts* you need to remember when you jog? Work with a partner. Make a chart.

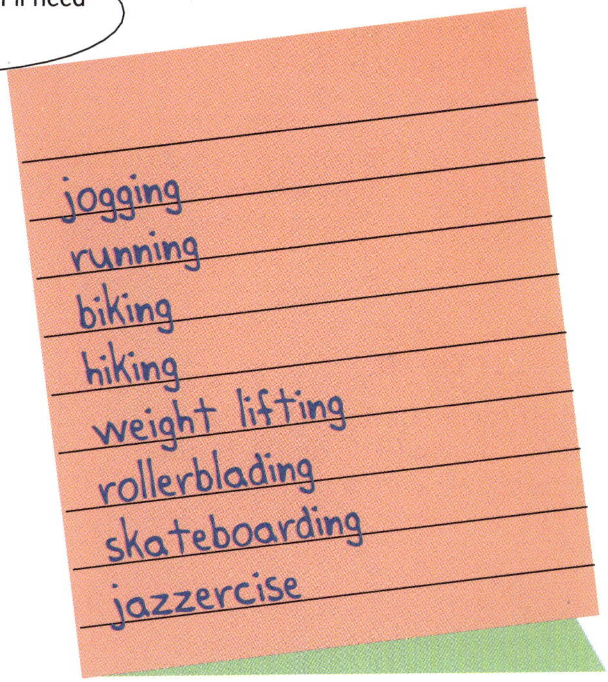

FIGURING IT OUT.

Match each item of clothing or equipment to an activity on Michelle's list.

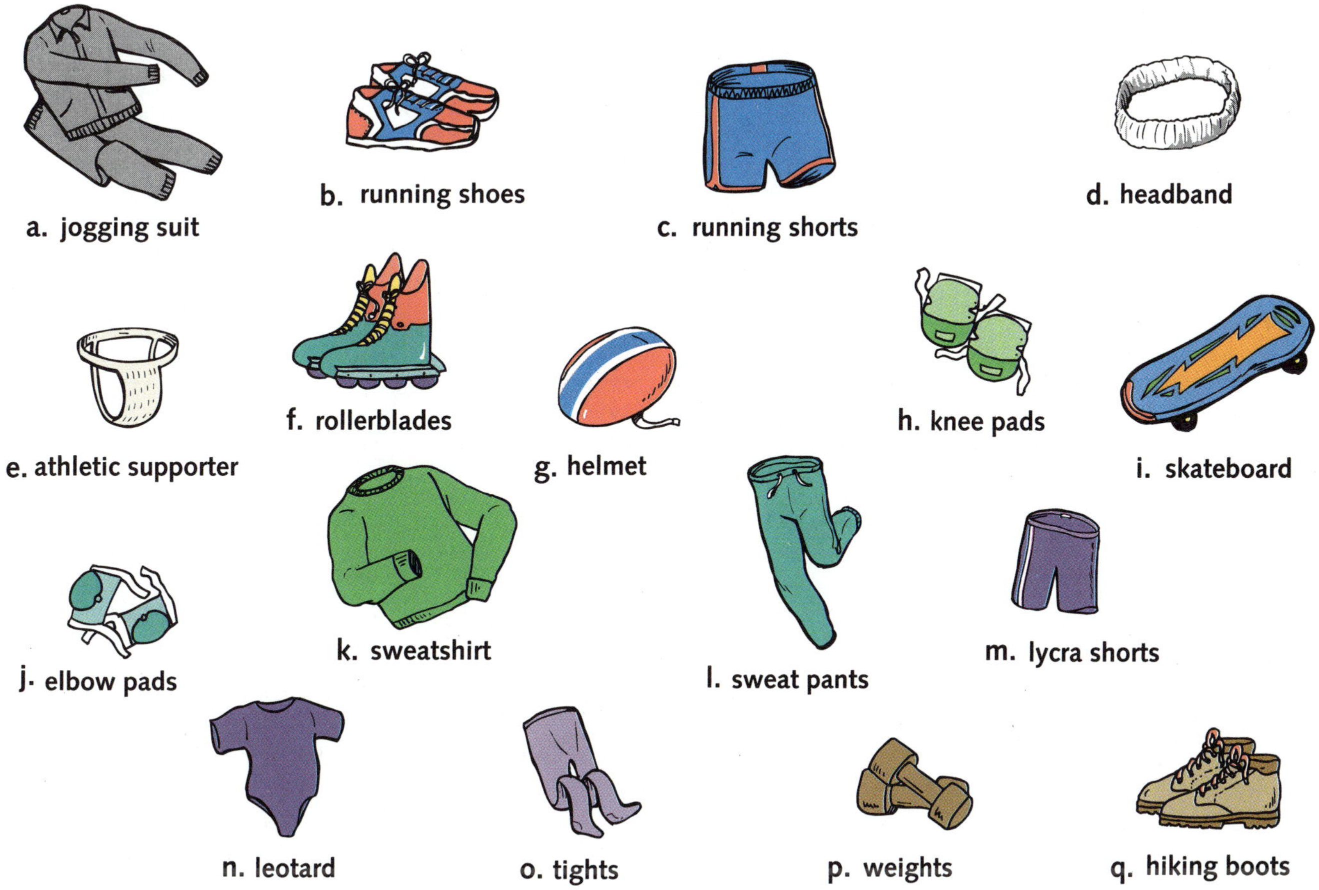

FINDING OUT. Work with a partner. Choose a sport or activity on Michelle's list. What one-time costs are involved in playing this sport or doing this activity? Are any ongoing costs involved? Estimate them.

LISTENING IN.

Why does Michelle say she feels a sore throat coming on?

TALKING IT OVER.

Read the fitness charts. How well do you think you would do on the health fitness test? Talk with a partner.

SIT-UPS

	AGE 11	12	13	14
BOYS				
Excellent	67	78	73	99
Good	50	51	54	60
Fair	30	37	40	44
Poor	23	28	30	33
GIRLS				
Excellent	50	50	50	49
Good	34	30	30	28
Fair	25	22	21	20
Poor	18	17	17	15

HEALTH FITNESS TEST

	KIDS MY AGE...	ME
How strong are my muscles?	See Performance-level Charts	?
How long can my muscles keep working?	The average kid can do 30 changes with each leg in one minute.	?
How flexible are my muscles?	Most kids can touch their toes without bending their knees.	?
What's my level of endurance?	Most kids can run between 1,200 and 1,400 yards in five minutes.	?
Do I have too much body fat?	The fold of skin under the navel should not be more than one inch.	?

FINDING OUT.

How physically fit are you? Ask your PE teacher to help you find out. Are there other fitness tests your teacher can suggest?

UNIT 11

THIS IS MY FAMILY!

TUNING IN. Listen to the rest of Ms. Tanaka's introduction. What will the broadcast cover? Use your own words.

LISTENING IN.

THINKING ABOUT IT.

Compare your own family to a TV family of your choice. In what ways are the two families the same? In what ways are they different? Fill in the chart.

	TV Family	My Family
Family member		
Who is in charge		
Family responsibilities		
How family members treat each other		
How family spends time together		
What makes the family interesting		

ON YOUR OWN.

A show about your own family is going to be on TV. Write a commercial that will make others want to watch the show.

THINKING ABOUT IT.

As you read Ms. Tanaka's descriptions of the various types of families, think about your own family. How would you describe it?

A lot of students live in what is called a *nuclear* family. A nuclear family consists of a father, a mother, and one or more children. Charles Kowalski is a member of a nuclear family.

More and more students at Kennedy, however, are members of *single-parent* families. A single-parent family has one parent and one or more children. David Fishman's parents were recently divorced. David lives with his mother.

And there is the *extended* family. It includes one or more relatives in addition to parents and children. Lori Chan is a member of an extended family that includes her mother and father, her two sisters, her grandmother, and her mother's sister.

Blended families are becoming more and more common. In a blended family, one or both of the parents have been married before and often have children from the previous marriage. Michelle Marais is a member of a blended family. Her mother married her stepfather three years ago, and Michelle now has a stepbrother in addition to a sister.

These are the types of families we find here at Kennedy. You'll get to know them better during the course of the broadcast.

TALKING IT OVER. Juan Ortíz lives with his uncle. Uncle Carlos is unmarried. Are Juan and his uncle a family? What are the characteristics of a family? Make a list.

TUNING IN. Listen as some of the students at Kennedy describe their families. What type of family is each?

TALKING IT OVER. How are families changing?

For many generations, the typical family consisted of a father, a mother, and children. The father had a job and was responsible for supporting the family. The mother was a homemaker and was responsible for taking care of the home and children.

Many of today's families no longer fit this traditional mold. According to recent government figures, nearly eight out of ten mothers with children under the age of 18 have jobs outside the home.

Work with a partner. Discuss how these changes are making a difference in the daily lives of families.

HOUSEHOLD RESPONSIBILITY CHART

RESPONSIBILITIES	FAMILY MEMBERS		
	Name:	Name:	Name:
Earning money			
Buying food			
Cooking			
Cleaning			
Working in the yard			
Doing the laundry			
Taking care of a pet			
Fixing things			
Doing the dishes			

THINKING ABOUT IT.

Make a chart that shows each person's household responsibilities in your family. Which responsibilities are shared? Which are not shared? Share your chart with your classmates.

TALKING IT OUT.

Explain how you help at home.

LISTENING IN. What responsibilities do you have at home?

Ms. Tanaka: Tell me, now that you are in middle school, do you have more responsibilities at home? Are there things that older people used to do for you that you now do for yourself?

Lori: When I was in elementary school, Dad used to fix my breakfast. Now I make my own breakfast.

Michelle: In my house, Mom used to get my clothes ready. Now I have to iron my own clothes.

TALKING IT OUT. Now that you're in middle school, you have more family responsibilities. Make a list of things that older people in your family would do for you.

THINKING ABOUT IT.

Compare the lists boys in your class wrote with the lists girls wrote. Are there any interesting differences?

TUNING IN. Listen to Chip and Juan's conversation. What is daily life like at home for you?

LISTENING IN.

How do families spend time together?

Ms. Tanaka: It's important for families to spend time together. This is not always possible. What about your families? How much time do you spend together?

David: My parents are divorced. Mom's so busy now that we don't spend much time together. And I rarely see my father.

Chip: I guess I'm lucky. My family still spends a lot of time together. We like to talk, play games, or just be with each other.

TALKING IT OVER.

What did you use to do with your family when you were younger that you no longer do today?

THINKING ABOUT IT.

Each family has its own ideas of what is fun. Work with a partner. Make a chart that compares how your two families have fun. Why is it important for families to have fun together?

Family 1	*Family 2*

TALKING IT OVER. How would you respond to the survey?

Ms. Tanaka: How much time do you spend together with your parents?
Chip: Last summer we took a family vacation. All nine of us.
Ms. Tanaka: OK. But what about a typical day?
Chip: Well, we usually eat dinner together. I guess I'd say we spend about an hour together. Is that typical?
Ms. Tanaka: In a recent survey, researchers asked teenagers how much time their mothers or fathers spend with them during the day. Here is what they said.

	Less than 5 minutes	5 to 30 minutes	30 minutes to 1 hour	1 to 2 hours	3 to 4 hours
Time spent with mother each day	12%	29%	24%	19%	15%
Time spent with father each day	19%	32%	22%	15%	11%

FIGURING IT OUT.

Work with a partner. Suppose Ms. Tanaka wanted to present the information in the survey visually. How might she do this?

TUNING IN.

Listen as Chip tells about his family vacation. Be ready to share a story of your own about a memorable family vacation.

JUST FOR Fun

Make a poster entitled "Ten Tips for Surviving a Family Vacation."

LISTENING IN. What about family rules?

Ms. Tanaka: What about discipline? Would you say your parents are strict or lenient? Just for fun, I'd like you to role play for our audience.

Lori: So, I'm supposed to pretend that I'm my mother? Let's see. What would my mother say . . .

Michelle: That'll be fun! I wish I had some funny old clothes I could wear!

TUNING IN. Listen as Lori and Michelle act out their parts. Whose parent is most like your own?

TALKING IT OVER. Work with a partner. Make a diagram that shows the rules in your own family and in your partner's family. Compare your family rules.

LISTENING IN.

Why does Michelle feel sorry for herself?

Michelle: Poor me! I have to be in bed by ten! My brother gets to stay up until eleven.
Lori: But he's only two years older than you are! That's not fair!
Michelle: And I have to do the dishes before I can watch TV. My brother can watch TV whenever he wants.
Lori: Really? In my family none of us can watch TV until all the chores are done.
Michelle: I can't talk on the phone until I finish my homework. My brother has his own phone!
Lori: How incredibly unfair!
Michelle: My parents think I'm still a baby!
Lori: I think it's because you're a girl!

TALKING IT OVER.

A middle school student wrote this poem about being a teenager. Read the poem. Think of other examples of being caught in the middle.

Adult? I ask
Is that what I am?
When I do something good
my parents answer yes.
When I do something bad
my parents answer no.
What am I?
An adult or a child?
I am trusted
to watch the house for a day.
But never
a week or weekend.
Am I an adult,
or am I a child?
At the movies
I pay adult admission.
But for rated R films,
I am not admitted.
I ask again,
Is a teenager an adult or a child?

THINKING ABOUT IT.

Imagine that you are the parent of fourteen-year-old twins — a boy and a girl. What are your rules? Are they the same or different for both kids?

LISTENING IN.

What are your own family values?

Ms. Tanaka: Families often differ in their values. I understand that you've recently conducted a survey on values for your school newspaper.

Lori: Yes. Our survey included a list of "Traditional Values." We asked people to react to each value on a scale of 1 to 5.

Values Survey

	Very Important	Quite Important	Important	Not Too Important	Not Important
Standing up for what's right	5	4	3	2	1
Being tolerant of others	5	4	3	2	1
Pursuing happiness	5	4	3	2	1
Working hard	5	4	3	2	1
Honoring your parents	5	4	3	2	1
Being honest	5	4	3	2	1
Playing to win	5	4	3	2	1
Helping other people	5	4	3	2	1
Living life to the fullest	5	4	3	2	1
Being loyal to your country	5	4	3	2	1
Getting rich	5	4	3	2	1
Getting a good education	5	4	3	2	1

TALKING IT OVER.

Work with a partner. Discuss what each value on the survey means. Use your own words. Give examples. What values would you add to the survey?

THINKING ABOUT IT.

How would you respond to each item on the survey.

FINDING IT OUT.

Give the survey to the members of your own family.

- ▲ For each item on the survey, figure out the average score for your family.
- ▲ Rank the items in order of importance for your family.
- ▲ Compare the results with your classmates.

FINDING OUT.

Find a partner whose cultural background is different from yours. Make a chart that compares your two families.

QUESTIONS TO ASK	CULTURE 1	CULTURE 2
Who is a family? Who usually lives under one roof?		
Who is "in charge" of the family? Who decides what?		
What are some typical responsibilities of family members?		
How do parents show affection to other family members?		
How do parents discipline their children? What happens when a child does something wrong?		

THINKING ABOUT IT.

Personal and family values are often influenced by culture. Make a list of values that seem to be more important in your own culture than in U.S. culture. Compare your list with your classmates' lists.

JUST FOR Fun

Work in groups of three. Help Lisa plan future editions of "Teens Today."

▲ List three possible topics.
▲ As a group, decide on one possible topic that you think would be most interesting to others.
▲ Choose a person to interview.
▲ Write questions to ask this person.
▲ Write an imaginary entry for the program for a TV guide.
▲ Share your ideas and your interview questions with your classmates.

UNIT 12

THIS IS AN EMERGENCY!

TUNING IN. Listen in on the conversation just before the accident. Explain what happened to Chip.

LISTENING IN.

What happened to Chip?

Mr. Ruiz: Did you see what happened?
Lori: Juan did.
Juan: We were tossing the football …
Mr. Ruiz: You're not supposed to be tossing footballs in the quad.
Juan: I know. I'm sorry. Anyway, we were tossing the football, and it landed in the tree. I said, "Let's get the custodian," but Chip said, "No, I'll climb up."
Mr. Ruiz: How was he going to get up in the tree?
Juan: He told me to clasp my hands together and lift him up. And then he just fell. I guess he hit his head. Will he be OK?
Mr. Ruiz: I don't know. Let's call for help.

ON YOUR OWN.

An eyewitness account of an event makes the reader feel as though he or she was there at the scene. Write a report of an emergency you have witnessed.

1. ***Before you write***
   - ▲ Think about the people who were involved. Recall as many details about them as you can.
   - ▲ What about the time and place? Which details are important to describe?
   - ▲ Make a simple timeline that shows what happened.
2. ***Draft your report***
   - ▲ Begin by describing the setting.
   - ▲ Using your timeline, describe what happened.
   - ▲ Use details to make your report come alive.
3. ***Review and revise your report***
   - ▲ Does your report match what happened?
   - ▲ Is your report exciting to read?

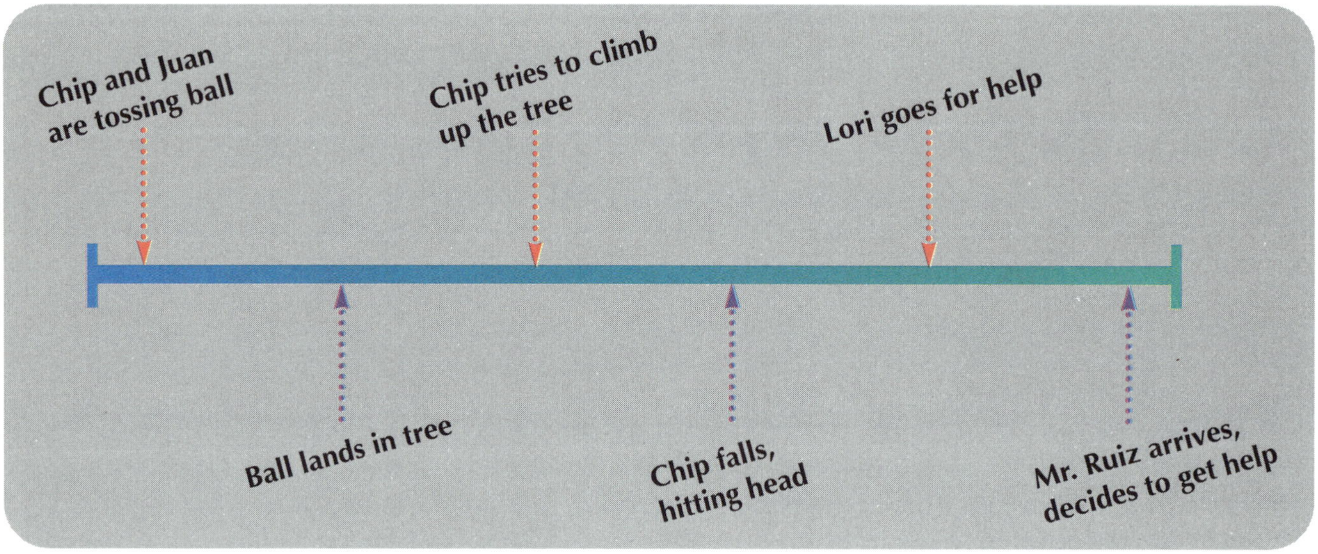

TALKING IT OVER.

When might each item in the first aid kit be useful?

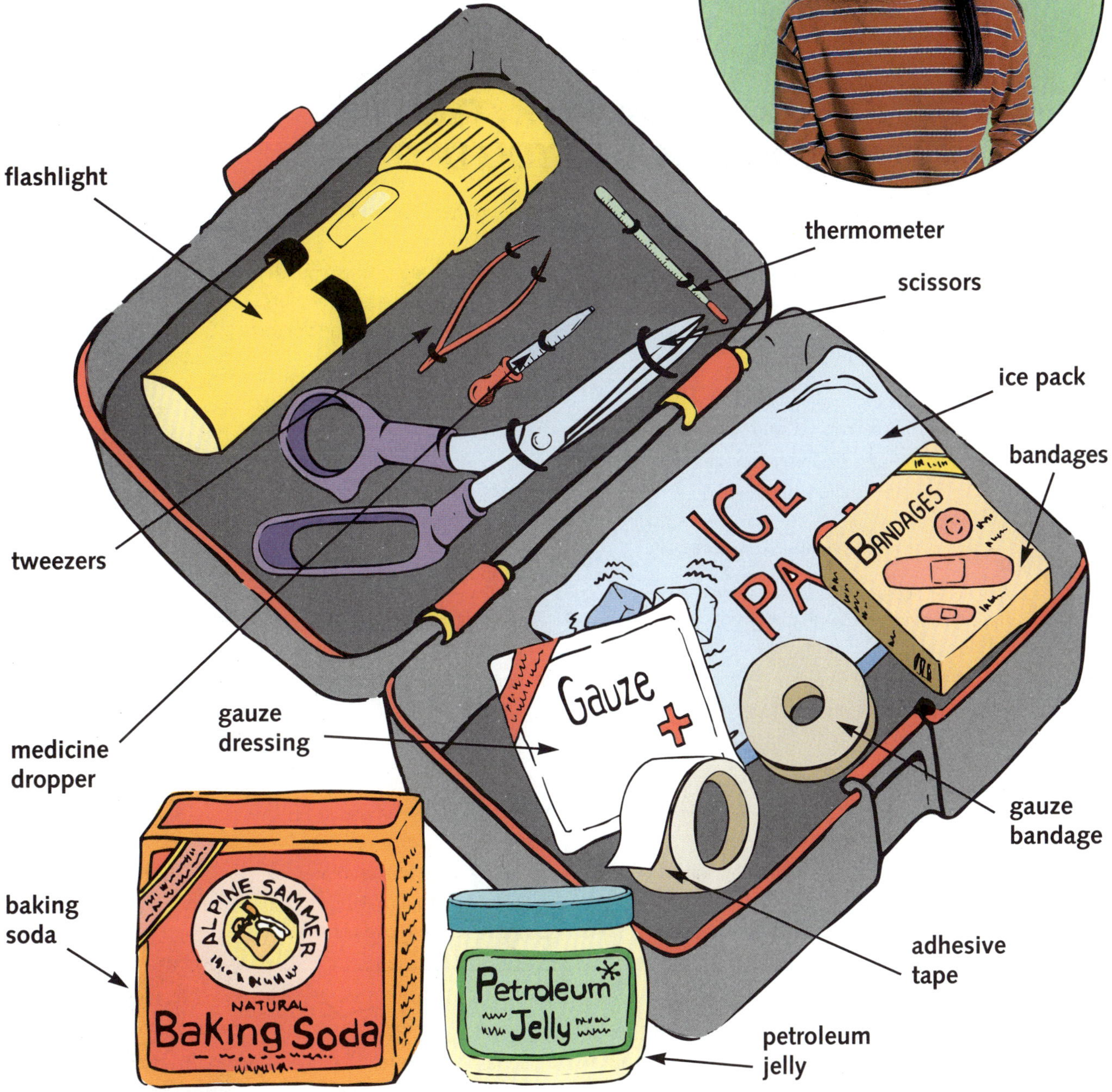

TUNING IN. Listen to each problem. Decide which item or items in the first aid kit you might need.

FINDING OUT. What other items do you often find in a first aid kit? Make a list.

ON YOUR OWN.

Do you know how to handle an emergency? Take the quiz. Share your answers with your classmates.

Medical Emergency Quiz
WHAT WOULD YOU DO?

1. Your brother begins to choke at the dinner table. Would you . . .
   a. pound him in the back until he stops choking?
   b. make him drink some water?
   c. do the Heimlich Maneuver?
2. Your father has cut his hand with a saw and is bleeding heavily. Would you . . .
   a. put a tourniquet around his wrist?
   b. apply pressure to the wound with a clean cloth?
   c. apply pressure to the nearest pressure point?
3. Your sister accidentally drinks some drain cleaner, thinking that it's milk. Would you . . .
   a. make her vomit?
   b. have her drink some water?
   c. call the poison-control center?
4. Your little sister puts her hand on a room heater. Her fingers are red and blistered. Would you . . .
   a. put her hand under cold running water?
   b. rub butter on the burns?
   c. pop the blisters with a pin?
5. Your brother is bitten by a stray dog. Would you . . .
   a. put a bandage on the wound?
   b. run after the dog and catch it?
   c. rush your brother to the doctor?
6. Your older brother is hit on the head by a baseball. It knocks him unconscious. Would you . . .
   a. keep him lying down and call for emergency help?
   b. wait until he wakes up, and then take him home?
   c. try to make him get up and walk around?
7. You are stung by a bee. The skin is red and beginning to swell. Would you . . .
   a. put baking soda or meat tenderizer on the bite?
   b. suck out the poison?
   c. pull out the stinger with tweezers?
8. Your father falls and breaks his arm. Would you . . .
   a. try to set the broken bone?
   b. keep him from moving and call for help?
   c. see if he can move his arm?

TUNING IN. Listen to the answers to the quiz. Which items did you answer correctly?

FINDING OUT. Work in a small group. Learn the first-aid procedures for one of the emergency situations pictured. Teach your classmates what you've learned.

1. 

2. 

3. 

4. 

5. 

6. 

7. 

8. 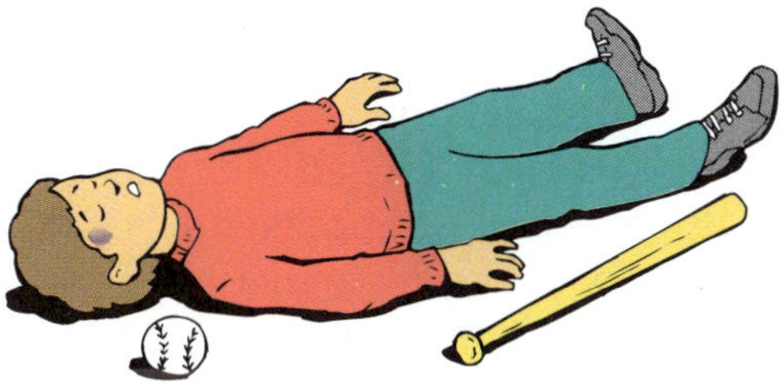

TALKING IT OVER. Imagine a major disaster such as a hurricane, tornado, or earthquake. What steps would you take to be prepared?

LISTENING IN. What do you know about safety and first aid?

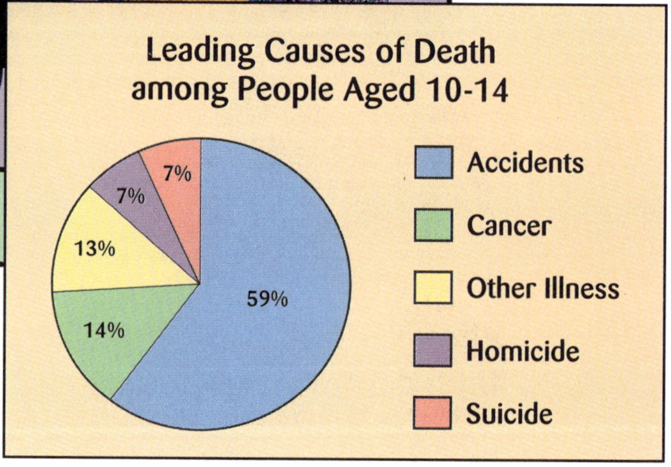

THINKING ABOUT IT.

According to the National Safety Council, accidents are the fourth leading cause of death in the United Sates. Why do you think accidents cause so many deaths, especially among teenagers? Why do you think accidents happen? Work with a partner. Make a chart like this one.

Common accidents	Why accidents happen

TALKING IT OUT. Have you ever witnessed an accident? What happened? What caused the accident?

Around 95,000 people in the U.S. die each year in accidents, according to the National Safety Council. Many fatal accidents happen at home.

TUNING IN.

Look at the statistics on accidental deaths. Listen to each statement. Point your thumb up if the statement is true. Point your thumb down if it is false.

FIGURING IT OUT.

Think of a visual way to present the statistics.

Leading Causes of Accidental Death in the U.S. Annually

Cause	Number killed
1. Auto accidents	46,900
2. Falls	12,400
3. Poisoning	6,500
4. Drowning	4,600
5. Fires	4,400
6. Choking	3,900
7. Firearms	1,600
8. Aircraft	817
9. Other causes	13,400

Source: U.S. Department of Commerce. Bureau of the Census.

Leading Causes of Death in Home Accidents in the Same Year

1. Falls	6,600
2. Poisoning	5,300
3. Drowning	600
4. Fires	3,300
5. Choking	2,700
6. Firearms	900
7. Other causes	3,100

Source: National Safety Council.

TALKING IT OVER.

Work with a partner. How could the number of deaths each year from accidents be reduced? Make a list of ideas.

1. Provide school safety programs
2.

TALKING IT OVER.

Identify the safety hazards in the picture.
How many accidents are waiting to happen?

FIRE PREVENTION TIPS

- Install one or more working smoke detectors.
- Develop and practice a home escape plan.
- Do not leave food cooking unattended.
- "Stop, Drop, and Roll" if your clothes are on fire.
- Store matches and lighters out of reach of children.
- Properly store flammable liquids.
- Beware of frayed electrical cords.

THINKING ABOUT IT.

Mr. Fields showed his students this fire safety poster. How safe is your own home or apartment? Do you have an emergency escape plan?

LISTENING IN. Do you know the Heimlich Maneuver?

1. Get behind the victim. Wrap your arms around the victim's waist.

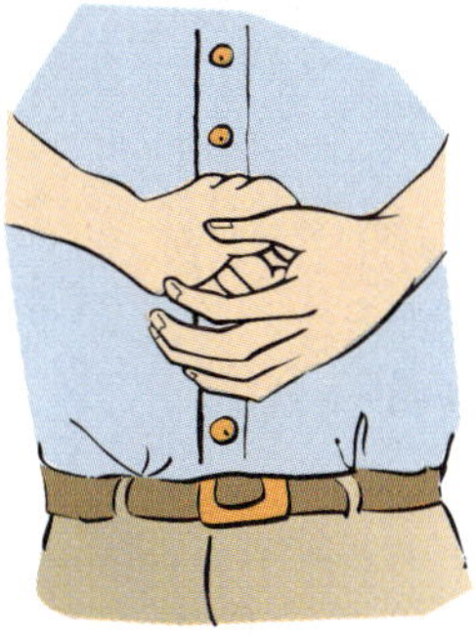

2. Make a fist with your right hand. Now grasp it with your left hand.

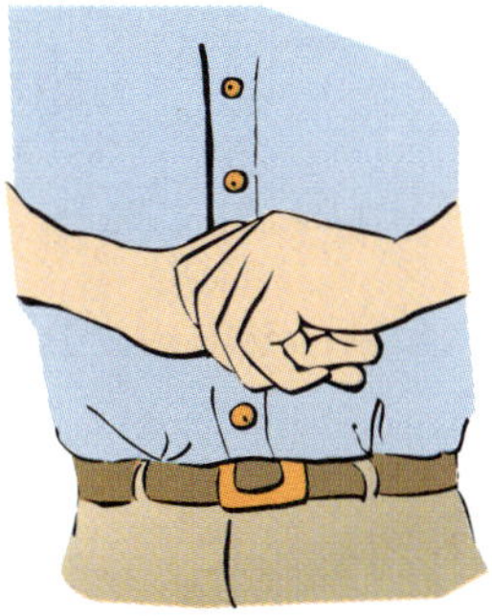

3. Place your fist on the victim's stomach, below the ribs and above the bellybutton.

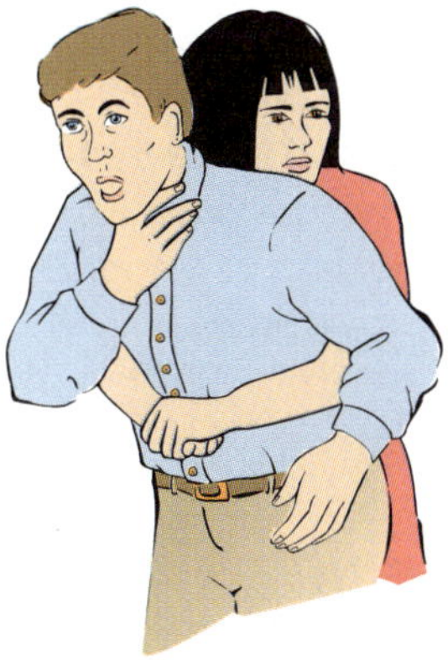

4. With a quick thrust upward, press your fist into the victim's stomach. This should force the food or object out of the airway. Repeat if necessary.

ACTING IT OUT. Pretend that one of your classmates is choking. Demonstrate the Heimlich Maneuver. Explain what you are doing. Use your own words.

LISTENING IN.

What would you do?

TALKING IT OVER.

Look in the cupboard and tell what each household product is used for. Which products does your family use?

FIGURING IT OUT.

Household products can be dangerous. The pictures show the harmful effects of household products. Work with a partner. Discuss which product or products can cause these symptoms.

makes you feel dizzy

makes you sick to your stomach

burns your eyes

burns your skin

kills you if you swallow it

LISTENING IN. Do you pay attention to the warnings on labels?

FINDING OUT. In many cases of poisoning, it is best to get the substance out of the victim's stomach as quickly as possible. But not always! Causing the victim to vomit can sometimes be harmful. For each poison, find out whether you should, or should not, induce vomiting. Make a chart.

ACTING IT OUT. Work with a partner. Imagine that your younger brother has swallowed a harmful household product. He was rushed to the emergency room. Explain the problem and the actions you've already taken to help.

FOLLOWING ALONG. You have an emergency at home. Do you know how to get help? Make an emergency phone call. Follow the directions.

1. Give the victim's location.

2. Tell what happened.

3. Give your name and phone number.

4. Give any other information that might help.

5. Ask questions and seek advice.

6. Always be the last person to hang up.

FINDING OUT. It's important to have information posted near your telephone that might be useful in an emergency. Make a list that includes the following entries. Then find out the phone number for each entry.

Home address Family doctor	Fire department Police department Ambulance service	Poison center Nearest relative or friend

TUNING IN. Listen to the 911 call. Then work with a partner. Make up your own 911 emergency telephone conversation. Act out the conversation for your classmates.

UNIT 13

YOU'RE OLD ENOUGH TO FIND A PART-TIME JOB!

Juan: Uncle Carlos, could you give me ten dollars?

Uncle Carlos: Ten dollars? Again? I can't afford giving you this kind of money! You're nearly fourteen. You're old enough to find a part-time job.

Juan: A job? I'm too young to have a job, and my English isn't good enough. What would I do?

Uncle Carlos: Don't make excuses. And your English is just fine. When I was your age, I was a paper carrier.

Juan: How will I find a job?

TUNING IN. Listen to the rest of the conversation. What do you think of Uncle Carlos's suggestions?

LISTENING IN.

Does Juan really need a part-time job?

Juan: I'd like to find a part-time job after school, Ms. Vasquez. My uncle suggested that I talk to you.
Ms. Vasquez: Why do you want a job? Are you sure you really need one?
Juan: I'd like to earn extra money.
Ms. Vasquez: Just keep in mind that if you have a job, your schoolwork may suffer. And you'll probably have less time for family and friends.
Juan: Hmmm. I haven't thought of that.
Ms. Vasquez: I'm not telling you not to work, but I am suggesting that you weigh the trade-offs before you decide.

THINKING ABOUT IT.

Work with a partner. Discuss the pros and cons of having a part-time job. Make a chart like this one.

Benefits of having a part-time job . . .	Drawbacks of having a part-time job . . .
• More income	• Less time for schoolwork

TALKING IT OVER.

This passage appeared in a magazine article on teenagers who work. What do you think?

. . . the desire for luxury consumer goods, rather than economic need, is the major reason that teenagers work. Many kids with jobs are struggling to keep up in school and they're spending their pay as quickly as they earn it. For the majority of teenagers, the value of working needs to be weighed against the payoff from other activities.

ON YOUR OWN. Suppose you really want to find a part-time job. Make a list of places you might look for job postings.

TUNING IN.

Listen to each statement about having a part-time job. Point your thumb up if you agree with the statement. Point your thumb down if you disagree.

FINDING OUT.

Find someone in your class who has a part-time job. Ask him or her some questions about the job.

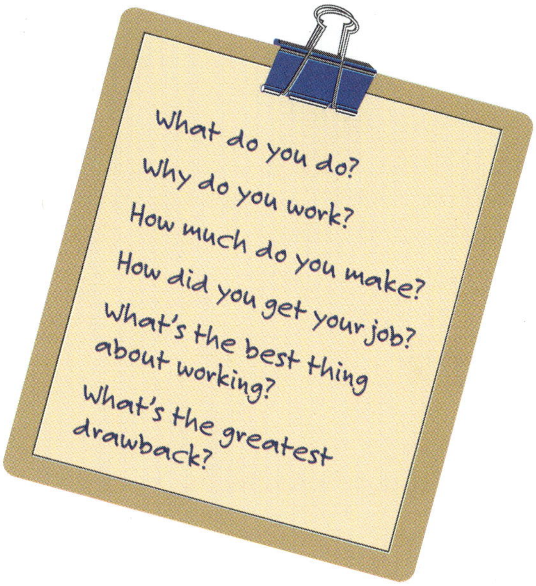

FIGURING IT OUT. You're offered a part-time job for ten hours a week. You can choose your own hours. Make a simple schedule that shows how you might balance school, your job, your friends, and your family obligations.

SUN	MON	TUES	WED	THURS	FRI	SAT

LISTENING IN. How do I find a job?

Juan: Suppose I want to work. How do I find a job?

Ms. Vasquez: The most important step is deciding what type of job might suit you.

Juan: You mean what I am interested in?

Ms. Vasquez: Right. If you like to be outdoors, then you might like yard work. But if you prefer being indoors, then you might like a job like babysitting. Let me ask you some questions about your interests and abilities.

POSSIBLE JOBS

1. Babysitting
2. Shoveling snow
3. Washing windows
4. Delivering newspapers
5. Doing yard work
6. Taking care of pets/walking dogs
7. Cleaning garages/basements
8. Painting house numbers on curbs
9. Housesitting
10. Making and selling handicrafts
11. Tutoring
12. Repairing bicycles, skateboards, etc.

TUNING IN.

Listen to Ms. Vasquez's questions and Juan's responses. Be ready to help Juan choose a job he might like.

TALKING IT OUT.

Suggest jobs that Juan might enjoy.

ON YOUR OWN.

Make a list of part-time jobs that would suit you, given your interests and abilities.

THINKING ABOUT IT. Think about experiences you've had that might help you find a part-time job. Include odd jobs, special school projects, clubs you've belonged to, and awards you've received. Make a chart like this one. Share your chart with your classmates.

Odd jobs	School Projects	Clubs/Organizations	Awards
Watched neighbor's apartment while on vacation	Helped plan book sale	Member of Ambassadors Club	Principal's Honor Roll

TALKING IT OUT. Look at Juan's list of possible jobs again. Add other jobs to the list. Tell your classmates which jobs would not suit you. Explain why!

I'm not strong enough.

I'm too disorganized.

I'm not old enough.
I'm not outgoing enough.
I'm not mature enough.

I'm too shy.
I'm too young.
I'm too inexperienced.

JUST FOR Fun

Make a list of jobs you think you might like to have when you're in high school. What kinds of experiences and abilities might help you get each of these jobs?

LISTENING IN.

What job has Juan chosen?

Juan: I've decided on a part-time job, Uncle Carlos. I've decided to try housesitting.

Uncle Carlos: Oh, really? I thought you were thinking of getting a paper route.

Juan: Well, I made a list of the advantages and disadvantages of some of the jobs I might like. Take a look.

TALKING IT OVER.

Discuss the advantages and disadvantages of each of the jobs on Juan's list.

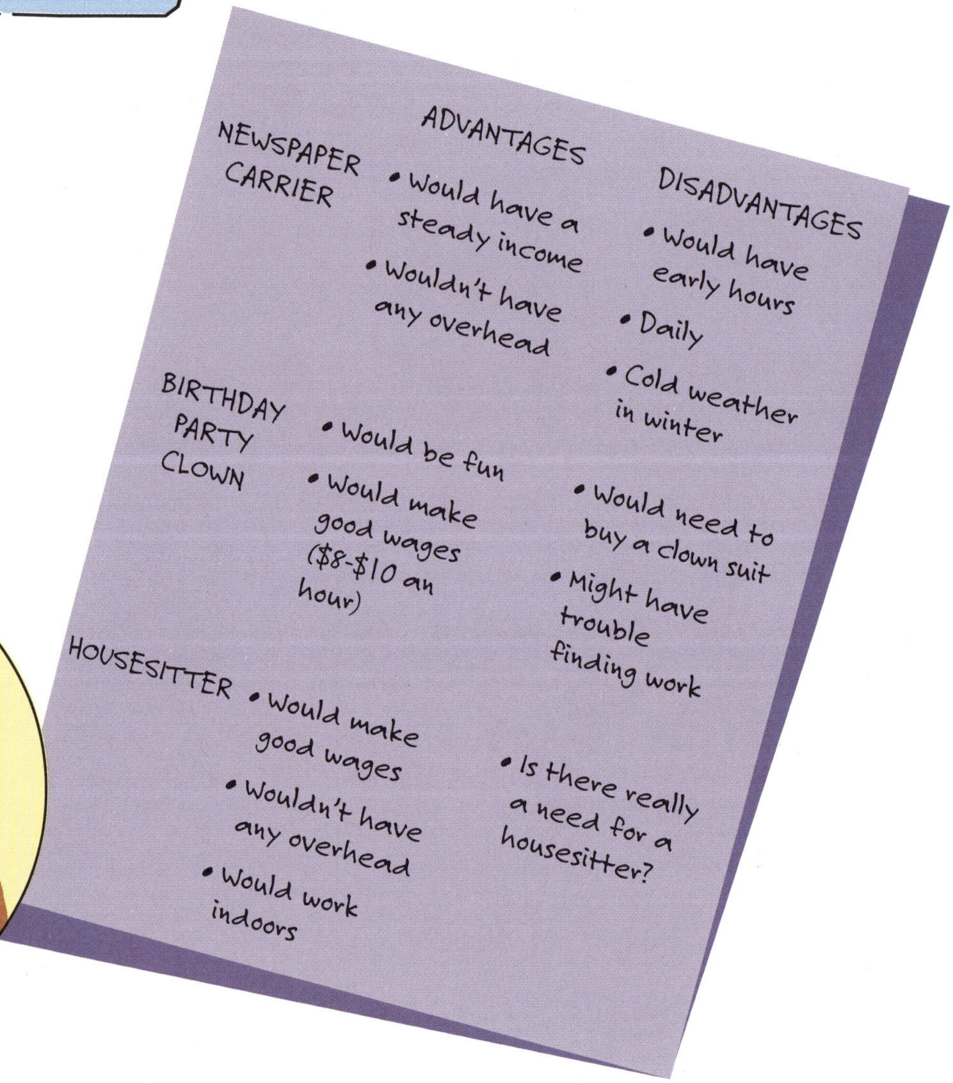

	ADVANTAGES	DISADVANTAGES
NEWSPAPER CARRIER	• Would have a steady income • Wouldn't have any overhead	• Would have early hours • Daily • Cold weather in winter
BIRTHDAY PARTY CLOWN	• Would be fun • Would make good wages ($8-$10 an hour)	• Would need to buy a clown suit • Might have trouble finding work
HOUSESITTER	• Would make good wages • Wouldn't have any overhead • Would work indoors	• Is there really a need for a housesitter?

FINDING OUT. Look at Juan's list of possible jobs again. How much do you think each job might pay? Make a guess for each job. Then check your guesses with people outside of class. Compare your findings with your classmates.

Are you going away on vacation or business?

Responsible teen will take care of your house or apartment while you're away.

Will provide the following services:

* Pet care
* Care of house plants/outdoor plants
* Daily inspection of interior and exterior of home

Call Juan
555-8921
Reliable * Low Rates

THINKING ABOUT IT.

Has Juan left off any important information on his flyer? Can you think of other services he might add? Are there any other additions he should make?

TALKING IT OVER.

Juan has decided to reach potential customers with a door-to-door flyer. Think of other ways he might market his services.

- putting a notice on the bulletin board at the market
- placing an ad in the neighborhood newspaper
- relying on word of mouth
-

JUST FOR Fun

New businesses sometimes use special promotions to get customers. Among other things they might use discount coupons, prizes, gifts, and other gimmicks. Talk with a partner. Think of a clever new way to promote Juan's service.

TALKING IT OVER.

Robert also wants to be a housesitter. Read the interview. If you were Mrs. Jackson, would you hire Robert?

Mrs. Jackson: I understand you are interested in looking after my apartment while I'm away, Robert.

Robert: Yeah, I could sure use the money.

Mrs. Jackson: Well, do you have any experience housesitting?

Robert: Not really. How hard can it be?

Mrs. Jackson: Do you have any other work experience?

Robert: Yeah, I used to babysit for the Smiths, but they didn't pay enough and the kids were brats so I quit.

Mrs. Jackson: I see. Let me tell you what I want done. I'd like you to check the apartment twice a day and . . .

Robert: Sorry. I can only make it once a day.

Mrs. Jackson: Well, thank you for coming over. I have another young man to interview. I'll call you if I need you.

TUNING IN. Now listen to Juan's interview with Mrs. Jackson. Who do you think will get the job? Explain why.

EIGHT INTERVIEWING TIPS

1. Dress neatly. Wear the neatest clothes you own.
2. Fill out the application neatly. Print clearly. Also, take your time.
3. Act grown up. Shake hands, look the interviewer in the eye, and stand up straight.
4. Show enthusiasm. Before you go to an interview, think of the reasons why you want the job. Tell the interviewer why you would like the job.
5. Go to the interview alone. Never bring along a friend.
6. Ask questions. Think of a few important questions in advance so you're prepared.
7. Don't worry if you feel nervous. Everyone gets nervous before job interviews. A little nervousness shows that it matters to you.
8. Don't be discouraged if you don't get the job. Sometimes you have to go on a lot of interviews until you find the right job.

FIGURING IT OUT.

Read the job interviewing tips for teens. Explain why Mrs. Jackson selected Juan rather than Robert.

TALKING IT OVER.

Suppose that Robert has asked you for advice on job interviewing skills. What feedback would you give him on his interview with Mrs. Jackson?

FIGURING IT OUT.

What you communicate with your body language in an interview is as important as what you say. What are each of these kids communicating?

1.

2.

3.

4.

5.

TALKING IT OUT.

What should Juan do or say in each situation?

1. The day after Mrs. Jackson leaves, her prize African violet starts to lose its leaves. The next day the blossoms fall off. Juan gives it more water. By the third day, the plant is nearly dead. What should Juan do?

2. Mrs. Jackson told Juan that she stopped the paper. The paper continues to arrive each morning, however. Juan decides to call the circulation office at the paper. What should he say?

3. Juan notices that something smells funny in the kitchen. He discovers that the refrigerator has stopped running and that the food inside is spoiling. What should he do?

4. Mrs. Jackson receives a bill from the power company. The bill is overdue. If the balance isn't paid within five days, the power will be turned off. What should Juan do?

5. Mrs. Jackson's neighbor stops Juan in the hallway. The neighbor tells him that her television is broken and that Mrs. Jackson has given her permission to watch her TV. She wonders if Juan might lend her the key to the apartment. What should Juan do?

TUNING IN. Mrs. Jackson has returned home. Listen as Juan explains what happened to her prized African violet. Would you accept his explanation?

ACTING IT OUT. Now pretend that you're Juan. What would you say? Work with a partner. Act out each situation.

1. Tell Mrs. Jackson about the problem with the paper and what you did about it.

2. Tell Mrs. Jackson about the refrigerator and what you did about it.

3. Tell Mrs. Jackson about the notice from the power company and how you solved the problem.

4. Tell Mrs. Jackson about the neighbor's request and what you did.

JUST FOR Fun

Work in groups of three or four. Think of a new problem for Juan. Decide how he should solve the problem. Write a short skit and act it out.

LISTENING IN. What has Juan learned?

Juan: Uncle Carlos, I've decided that I don't want a part-time job, after all. It's not worth it.
Uncle Carlos: Oh? What happened?
Juan: What didn't happen?
Uncle Carlos: At least you'll have more time for your homework.
Juan: That reminds me . . . Yes. I have to write a personal narrative for ESL. It's due tomorrow. Now I know what to write about.

ON YOUR OWN.

Writing a personal narrative is a good way to share an important event or experience in your life. Follow these steps.

I was the luckiest kid in town! I had found the ideal part-time job. What could be easier than looking after our neighbor Mrs. Jackson's apartment? As I unlocked her front door, I said to myself, "This will be a piece of cake! What can possibly go wrong?" I was about to find out.

1. ***Decide what you will write about***
   - ▲ Look through your journal or notebook for ideas. A story that involves a conflict or problem will be especially worth telling.
   - ▲ Write down important details about what happened, who was involved, and where the event took place.
2. ***Draft your narrative***
   - ▲ Begin by setting the "stage." Describe the setting or situation.
   - ▲ Tell what happened in chronological order.
   - ▲ Use dialog to make your story more dramatic.
   - ▲ If there was a conflict, end your story by telling how the conflict was resolved.
3. ***Review and revise your narrative***
   - ▲ Does your narrative tell what happened? Will your reader be able to follow the events?
   - ▲ Is your narrative interesting to read?

UNIT 14

MAYBE YOU SHOULD RUN FOR OFFICE!

Lori: I'm mad!
Michelle: What's wrong?
Lori: Our school has so many problems these days.
Michelle: Like what?
Lori: Fighting, stealing, graffiti in the bathrooms . . .
Michelle: Maybe you should run for office in next month's school elections!
Lori: What good would that do?
Michelle: Well, if you were on the Student Council, you could suggest ideas to make our school better.
Lori: You're right! I could run on a "Do Right!" platform — just like they did at Washington High School.
Michelle: A "Do Right!" platform? What's that? What do you mean?

TUNING IN. Listen to the rest of Lori and Michelle's conversation. In your own words, explain Lori's "Do Right!" platform.

THINKING ABOUT IT.

This chart shows how Kennedy's school government is organized. How does the organization of this Student Council compare to the one at your school?

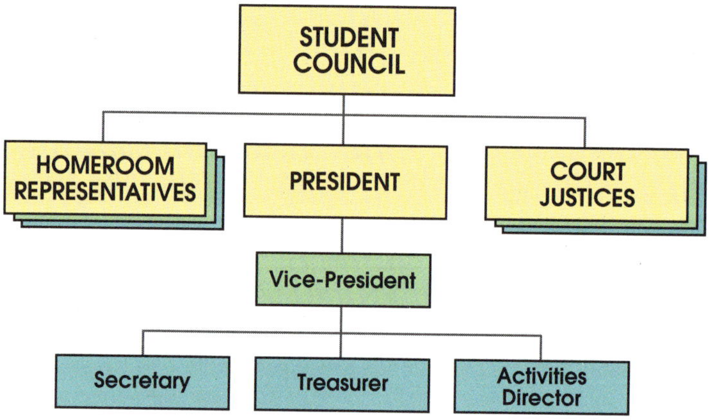

STUDENT COUNCIL RESPONSIBILITIES

- ▲ Makes recommendations to principal
- ▲ Decides how to spend student funds
- ▲ Plans Student Council activities

Offices	Officeholders	Responsibilities

FINDING OUT.

Who are your Student Council officers? What are their responsibilities? Make a chart.

JUST FOR Fun

Hold your own class elections! Work with your classmates. Follow these steps.

- ▲ First decide what kinds of officers your class needs.
- ▲ Next decide what the duties of each officer should be.
- ▲ Then nominate at least three people for each class office.
- ▲ Finally decide on a date for your election.

ON YOUR OWN. Find out when and where the next Student Council meeting takes place. Attend a meeting.

LISTENING IN. Which office should Lori run for?

READING ABOUT IT.

Read about the responsibilities of the Kennedy Student Council officers. Then look at the chart you made for your school's Student Council officers. Are some of the officers' responsibilities the same? Are some different?

RESPONSIBILITIES OF ELECTED OFFICERS

Officer	*Duties*
President	Represents our school Leads Student Council meetings Represents Council in meetings with the principal Serves on Parent-Teacher-Student Association
Vice-president	Carries out duties of president if president is absent
Secretary	Takes minutes of Council meetings
Treasurer	Is responsible forStudent Council funds
Student Activities Director	Plans extracurricular student activities
Homeroom Representatives	Make recommendations to the principal Approve budget Represent homerooms in Council meetings
Court Justices	Settle disputes Interpret school constitution May help decide certain discipline cases

TALKING IT OVER.

Lori would like to see many changes at her school. What office should she run for? Talk with a partner. Then share your ideas with your classmates.

THINKING ABOUT IT.

List reasons why someone might run for Student Council president.

TUNING IN. What would you do if you were elected Student Council president? Listen to Lori's ideas. Point your thumb up if you agree with an idea. Point your thumb down if you disagree.

Daily Bulletin

Tuesday, May 10 — John F. Kennedy Middle School

Three Enter Race for Student Council President

Three candidates announced yesterday that they are candidates for Student Council president at Kennedy Middle School. Elections will take place on June 7. Two seventh graders and one sixth grader are in the race.

Seventh grader Lori Chan is running on a "Do Right!" platform, which stresses personal honesty and responsibility to others. As a sixth grader, she served on the Student Council as a Homeroom Representative. She is on the Principal's Honor Roll and is a member of the Languages and Cultures Club.

Seventh grader John Banducci promises to be a friend to the athletics program. He currently serves as Student Council Activities Director and is active in Kennedy's after-school sports program. His favorite sport is football.

Sixth grader David Fishman is running on a "pro-student" platform. He opposes homework, would like to see the school day shortened, and vows to fight for a candy machine for the school cafeteria.

Sixteen candidates are running for other offices.

In addition to selecting school officers, students will also vote on four ballot measures.

- Measure A would raise Student Council card fee to $4.
- Measure B would authorize the expenditure of student funds on an end-of-the-year picnic.
- Measure C would ban the sale of candy on campus.
- Measure D would change the school mascot from the cougar to the lion.

READING ALOUD.

Pretend that it is your job to read the school bulletin to your classmates over the intercom. Read the bulletin in a way that makes it interesting to others.

TUNING IN.

Listen to the statements about the upcoming election. Hold up one finger for statements of fact. Hold up two fingers for opinions.

THINKING ABOUT IT.

Work with a partner. Imagine that the proposed measures are on the ballot at your school. What are the pros and cons of each proposal? How would you vote? Make a chart.

	Pros	Cons	My vote
Measure A			
Measure B			
Measure C			
Measure D			

LISTENING IN. The candidates are giving campaign speeches. Do their speeches tell you anything new about them?

PROFILE
Lori Chan
7th grader
Former 6th-grade Homeroom Representative
Principal's Honor Roll
Active in Languages and Cultures Club
Philosophy: "Leadership through service to others!"

PROFILE
John Banducci
7th grader
Current Activities Director
Active in after-school sports teams
Philosophy: "Go for it!"

PROFILE
David Fishman
6th grader
Member of Science Club
No previous elective office
Philosophy: Declined to state

THINKING ABOUT IT.

Work with a partner. Based on what you heard and read about the candidates, what do you think are the strengths and weaknesses of each one? Make a chart. Who would you vote for?

Candidate	Strengths	Weaknesses
Lori Chan		
John Banducci		
David Fishman		

JUST FOR Fun

Work in small groups. Brainstorm measures to propose to the rest of the class. After each group has shared its proposals, select three that will appear on a class ballot.

LISTENING IN.

Do you think Chip will make a good campaign manager? Why or why not?

Lori: I'm glad you've agreed to be my campaign manager, Chip.
Chip: You'll need publicity. You have to convince the voters! You'll need a slogan.
Lori: How about "Lori Chan . . . a voice for change!"
Chip: Maybe. You'll need to convince people that you're the most qualified.
Lori: I have lots of experience.
Chip: And you'll need to prove that you're a leader.
Lori: I know that I'll do a great job.
Chip: And that you'll stand for something.
Lori: I support the "Do Right!" platform.
Chip: And, remember, we have to follow Kennedy's campaign rules and procedures.

TALKING IT OVER.

Read the campaign rules and procedures. Would you add any other rules to Kennedy's policy? Describe them.

KENNEDY CAMPAIGN RULES AND PROCEDURES

1. No candidate may accept campaign contributions.
2. Posters may only be posted on school bulletin boards and in the quad.
3. Candidates may not disrupt classrooms.
4. Posters must be removed after elections.
5. Teachers may not give candidates special treatment.
6. Negative campaigning is not allowed.

JUST FOR Fun

Make a campaign poster for one of the measures on your class ballot. Remember that your poster should convince people to vote "for" or "against."

THINKING ABOUT IT. Match each of Lori's statements with a characteristic of an effective leader. Do you think she would make a good president?

SEVEN QUALITIES OF AN EFFECTIVE LEADER

1. Confident
2. Motivated
3. Hard working
4. Responsible
5. Takes initiative
6. Persevering
7. Caring

LISTENING IN. Why is Lori talking to the voters?

SPEAKING UP!

What are you for?
What are you against?

LISTENING IN. Why is Neelam taking an election poll?

Neelam: I'm taking an election poll for the school paper. Who are you voting for for president?
Tran: John Banducci!
Michelle: Lori Chan!
Neelam: Why?
Tran: He's smarter than she is!
Michelle: No he isn't! Lori's as smart as John is.
Tran: John's got a better sense of humor. He's funnier!
Michelle: Well, Lori's more responsible. And she'll work harder!

TUNING IN. Decide whether each statement you hear about the candidates is a fact or an opinion. Hold up one finger for facts. Hold up two fingers for opinions.

TALKING IT OVER.

Describe Lori and John.

athletic	intelligent
capable	loving
confident	popular
energetic	serious
friendly	strong
happy	talented
hard-working	trustworthy

JUST FOR Fun

Conduct your own poll on the measures on your class ballot. Make a chart to summarize the results.

KENNEDY ELECTION POLL RESULTS

President

Banducci	26%
Chan	26%
Fishman	12%
Undecided	36%

Measure A: Would raise Student Council card fee to $4.

• Favor	26%
• Oppose	26%
• Undecided	48%

Measure B: Would spend student funds on school picnic.

• Favor	96%
• Oppose	3%
• Undecided	1%

Measure C: Would ban the sale of candy on campus.

• Favor	35%
• Oppose	38%
• Undecided	27%

Measure D: Would change the school mascot from a cougar to a lion.

• Favor	10%
• Oppose	80%
• Undecided	10%

FIGURING IT OUT.

Present information from the poll results using different forms. Here is an example.

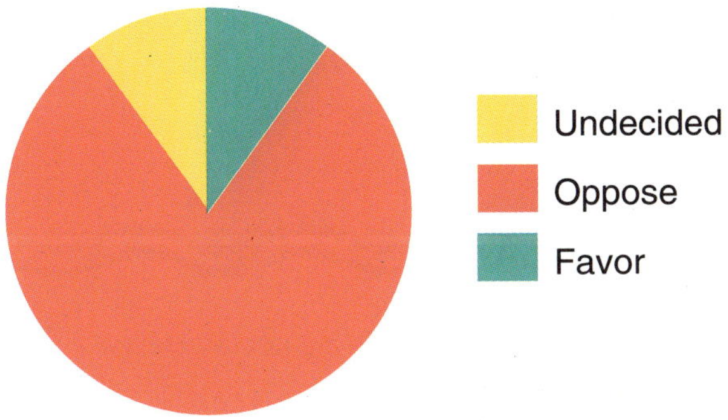

Measure D

TALKING IT OVER.

Look at the election poll results. What do the results reveal? Use the words in the box.

Most kids are for . . .	Hardly anyone is for . . .
Many are for . . .	Only a few are for . . .
Some are for . . .	Almost nobody is for . . .
A few kids are for . . .	Nearly everyone is for . . .

LISTENING IN.

Do you think Lori is nervous?

Chip: It's election day! Are you nervous, Lori?
Lori: Yes, but I think I'll win!
Chip: You have a good attitude.
Lori: You know the saying "Believe in yourself, because at times you might be the only one who will."

TALKING IT OUT.

Explain how to vote. Use your own words.

1.

Sign the voter register.

2.

Pick up a ballot.

3.

Enter the voting booth.

4.

Read the ballot carefully.

5.

Put an X in the box next to each of your choices.

6.
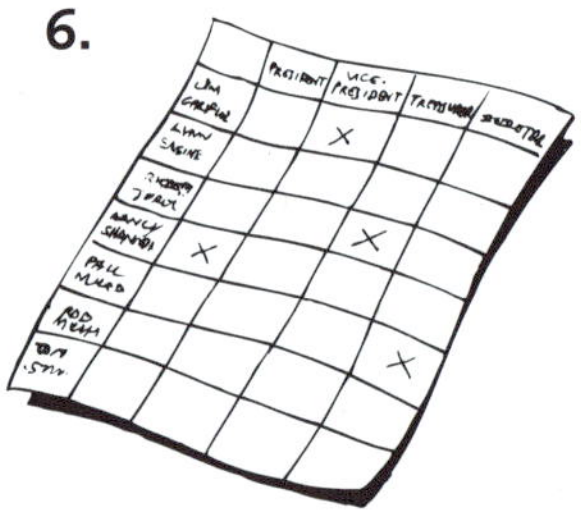
Only vote for one candidate for each office.

7.

Check over your ballot.

8.

Drop your ballot in the ballot box.

JUST FOR Fun

Hold your own class election. Make sure that the voting is by secret ballot. Decide who should count the votes.

LISTENING IN.

Did all of the Kennedy students vote in the election?

Ms. Goldstein:	We had a good turnout this year!
Juan:	How many kids voted?
Ms. Goldstein:	More than usual. Here are the figures. Let's make a graph. Let's also look at voting trends over the past five years.

THINKING ABOUT IT.

This column graph shows how many students voted in the election. Explain what the graph says. Use your own words.

	Eligible voters	Number who voted
6th grade	320	241
7th grade	331	220
8th grade	304	180

	Total eligible voters	Number who voted
This year's elections	955	641
Last year's elections	922	544
Two years ago	899	468
Three years ago	880	440
Four years ago	873	435

FIGURING IT OUT. Work with a partner. Make a graph that shows five-year voting patterns at Kennedy Middle School. Use the information in the table.

LISTENING IN. Why can't the students hear the results?

TUNING IN. Listen as Mr. Ruiz reads the results over the PA system. Report the results in your own words.

JUST FOR Fun

Have a victory celebration for the winners of your class election.

My Journal

My Journal

My Journal

My Journal

My Journal

My Journal